New Directions for
Higher Education

Betsy O. Barefoot
Jillian L. Kinzie
Co-editors

Developing and Assessing Personal and Social Responsibility in College

Robert D. Reason
EDITOR

Number 164 • Winter 2013
Jossey-Bass
San Francisco

DEVELOPING AND ASSESSING PERSONAL AND SOCIAL RESPONSIBILITY IN COLLEGE
Robert D. Reason
New Directions for Higher Education, no. 164
Betsy O. Barefoot and Jillian L. Kinzie, Co-editors

Microfilm copies of issues and articles are available in 16mm and 35mm, as well as microfiche in 105mm, through University Microfilms Inc., 300 North Zeeb Road, Ann Arbor, MI 48106-1346.

NEW DIRECTIONS FOR HIGHER EDUCATION (ISSN 0271-0560, electronic ISSN 1536-0741) is part of The Jossey-Bass Higher and Adult Education Series and is published quarterly by Wiley Subscription Services, Inc., A Wiley Company, at Jossey-Bass, One Montgomery Street, Suite 1200, San Francisco, CA 94104-4594. POSTMASTER: Send address changes to New Directions for Higher Education, Jossey-Bass, One Montgomery Street, Suite 1200, San Francisco, CA 94104-4594.

New Directions for Higher Education is indexed in Current Index to Journals in Education (ERIC); Higher Education Abstracts.

Individual subscription rate (in USD): $89 per year US/Can/Mex, $113 rest of world; institutional subscription rate: $311 US, $351 Can/Mex, $385 rest of world. Single copy rate: $29. Electronic only–all regions: $89 individual, $311 institutional; Print & Electronic–US: $98 individual, $357 institutional; Print & Electronic–Canada/Mexico: $98 individual, $397 institutional; Print & Electronic–Rest of World: $122 individual, $431 institutional.

Editorial correspondence should be sent to the Co-editor, Betsy O. Barefoot, Gardner Institute, Box 72, Brevard, NC 28712.

Cover photograph © Digital Vision

www.josseybass.com

CONTENTS

EDITOR'S NOTES

In an open letter to her students, Melissa Harris-Perry, MSNBC television host and Tulane University professor of political science, suggested that voting was "the citizenship equivalent of brushing your teeth: I am glad you do it regularly, but I am hardly going to applaud you for achieving such a minimal responsibility" (2011, para. 1). Unfortunately, voting behavior is often the primary outcome in research and writing related to civic learning and democratic engagement. This attention on voting casts an overly narrow scope on what it means to be an active and engaged member of a democracy.

The Association of American Colleges and Universities (AAC&U) began the Core Commitments Initiative in 2007, long before Dr. Harris-Perry likened voting to toothbrushing but for similar reasons: AAC&U saw the need to expand the conversation among higher educators to include more than simply voting behaviors. The Core Commitments Initiative focused the discussion on the broader concept of *personal and social responsibility (PSR)* with the understanding that such a focus would not only be more inclusive but also return higher education in the United States to its historical roots. Expanding the conversation to emphasize PSR leaves room for behavioral measures, like voting or hours spent in community service, and also opens our understanding of citizenship to include issues of civic identity, civic attitudes, personal integrity, and ethics. This broader conceptualization is the focus of this volume.

This volume explores the research and practice related to PSR as an outcome of college, focusing intentionally on how institutions can facilitate the development of PSR in the students enrolled in their institutions. After this short introductory preface, the first four chapters lay the foundation upon which the good practice chapters that follow are built. These chapters address the theoretical rationales for including PSR as an intentional outcome of college, the existing empirical research that suggests good practices, and the issues associated with assessing PSR. This initial section focuses on creating a sense of institutional pervasiveness (a campus climate) that encourages student development of PSR.

Caryn McTighe Musil, a senior scholar and director of Civic Learning and Democracy Initiatives at AAC&U, provides a theoretical and philosophical justification for AAC&U's focus on personal and social responsibility.

In Chapter 2, Robert D. Reason, Andrew J. Ryder, and Chad Kee review the existing empirical literature related to PSR, answering two broad questions: why educate for PSR and what are the challenges to educating for PSR. The authors also use the existing empirical research to link education

NEW DIRECTIONS FOR HIGHER EDUCATION, no. 164, Winter 2013 © Wiley Periodicals, Inc.
Published online in Wiley Online Library (wileyonlinelibrary.com) • DOI:10.1002/he.20070

for PSR to other important outcomes of higher education, making the case for the importance of studying PSR. This literature review lays the foundation for a greater understanding of how colleges and universities can influence the development of PSR among their students—the themes of the final three chapters in this volume.

In Chapter 3, Carol Trosset, of Bennington College, challenges higher educators and higher education researchers to think more broadly about PSR. Trosset argues that even with AAC&U's broad definition of PSR, the existing literature is overly focused on those behaviors that most logically would be categorized as *social responsibility*, practically ignoring more personal forms of responsibility. Trosset calls on researchers to include more emphasis on academic integrity and fulfilling one's personal responsibilities in family and work situations to our research agendas.

Chapter 4, by Andrew J. Ryder and Joshua J. Mitchell, moves the conversation to focus on issues of assessment related to PSR, specifically emphasizing issues related to assessing learning climates but including other outcome measures. This chapter introduces the Personal and Social Responsibility Inventory (PSRI) and serves as a bridge to focusing on what has been learned from the work of the Core Commitments Initiative. The PSRI is a climate assessment that emerged from the work of the Core Commitments Initiative and is available for institutional use through Iowa State University's Research Institute for Studies in Education.

The succeeding chapters build upon the work of higher education institutions that participated in the AAC&U's Core Commitments Initiative. These chapters interweave examples drawn from the experiences of these institutions to address good practices meant to intentionally infuse PSR in coursework and the cocurriculum. Each chapter highlights those practices that integrate curricular and cocurricular experiences in a holistic approach to the development of PSR. A final chapter in this section addresses how administrators can remove institutional obstacles to the infusion of PSR into the institutional ethos.

Nancy O'Neill, who served at AAC&U during the Core Commitments Initiative and now works at the University of Baltimore, focuses on good practices for infusing personal responsibility into the curriculum and cocurriculum. O'Neill draws examples from Core Commitments institutions that focused specifically on issues of academic integrity and ethical behavior. Robert D. Reason, director of the PSRI and a faculty member at Iowa State University, focuses the next chapter on institutional initiatives related to infusing social responsibility into students' experiences.

The final chapter, written by Chris R. Glass, assistant professor at Old Dominion University, draws upon a qualitative research project to identify good practices for the institutionalization of PSR as essential foci of the college experience. Glass draws upon interviews and seven institutional case studies to provide readers with a road map to begin to infuse PSR into their curriculum and cocurriculum. Glass builds upon the previous two chapters and integrates an understanding of organizational behavior to highlight strategies that begin to make permanent the focus on PSR.

The work of this volume and the reinvigorated emphasis on PSR would not have been possible without AAC&U's ongoing commitment to liberal education for college students in the United States, particularly the work of those associated with the Core Commitments Initiative. The Core Commitments staff included leadership by Caryn McTighe Musil, L. Lee Knefelkamp, Nancy O'Neill, and Michele Leaman. The PSRI was originally created by L. Lee Knefelkamp, Lauren Ruff, and Richard Hersh, and ultimately refined by the late Eric Dey and the graduate students from the University of Michigan: Mary Antonaros, Cassie Barnhardt, Matthew A. Holsapple, and Molly C. Ott.

Most important, this volume would not have been possible without the energy of the 23 Core Commitment Leadership Consortium institutions who participated in the yearlong dialogue on their campuses. We drew upon the work of these institutions and the lessons learned to inform the final chapters of this volume. We owe a debt of gratitude to those higher educators who spoke with us and shared their learning.

Robert D. Reason
Editor

Reference

Harris-Perry, M. (2011, January 10). In the wake of the tragedy in Arizona: An open letter to my students. *The Nation.* Retrieved from http://www.thenation.com/blog/157608/wake-tragedy-arizona-open-letter-my-students

ROBERT D. REASON *is associate professor of higher education at Iowa State University and director of the Personal and Social Responsibility Inventory.*

1

This chapter provides an overview of the Core Commitments Initiative conducted by the Association of American Colleges and Universities (AAC&U). Core Commitments was intended to reinvigorate the conversation about personal and social responsibility within higher education, and served as the impetus for this New Directions volume.

Overview of the Core Commitments Initiative

Caryn McTighe Musil

"It isn't so much a certain type of program that I have in mind, but an entire ethos of ethical responsibility for the nation's greater good that ought to be pervasive in the atmosphere of learning at every college and university in this land. ... Societal responsibility, as opposed to purely mercenary individual self-interest, ought to be part of the curriculum itself—and more than the curriculum, it ought to be part of the milieu ... of academic education."

Jonathan Kozol (as cited in Carlson, 2009, "A Question for the President," para. 4)

Jonathan Kozol's civic vision of higher education offers a stark contrast to the reductionist view of colleges as employment training schools whose curriculum should be tied only to preparing students to fill immediate job vacancies in a given state. It is also a stark contrast to the conversation in which some research centers and governors are recommending tracking and rewarding universities and colleges that secure graduates high-paying jobs. One governor even proposed penalizing low-paying majors by charging students higher tuition for specializing in, say, religion or English or social work. Such narrow preparation, driven disproportionately by jobs and salaries, risks stripping students of a powerful liberal education that evidence suggests will serve both them and the public well over a lifetime. The Core Commitments Initiative, and this edited volume that arose from the work of Core Commitments, is an antidote to educating students for narrow self-interest. Instead, it reminds readers why education for social responsibility should be at the epicenter of every student's college education.

New Directions for Higher Education, no. 164, Winter 2013 © Wiley Periodicals, Inc.
Published online in Wiley Online Library (wileyonlinelibrary.com) • DOI:10.1002/he.20071

In his book, *Ethical Leadership: The Quest for Character, Civility, and Community*, Walter Earl Fluker (2009) writes, "Leaders of the new century must not only be aware of environmental realities that shape the challenges and issues that they must confront. They must also be aware of the inner environments that shape character, civility, and a sense of community" (p. vii). He goes on to ask, "What are the critical resources and methodologies at our disposal to develop a new generation of emerging leaders who are awake—physically and emotionally whole, spiritually disciplined, intellectually astute, and morally anchored?" Two years earlier, the Association of American Colleges and Universities (AAC&U, 2007) sought to make such questions paramount in higher education when it issued its report, *College Learning for the New Global Century*. Moving from a paradigm that measured learning by the number of course credits to one that relied on what students know and could actually do, AAC&U's report laid out a growing consensus across 2- and 4-year colleges and universities about four essential learning outcome quadrants. One of those four was personal and social responsibility (PSR).

The PSR outcome includes civic knowledge and engagement, both locally and globally; diversity and global knowledge and intercultural competence; ethical reasoning and action; and foundations and skills for lifelong learning. Achieving such learning is typically anchored in active involvement with diverse communities and real-world challenges. Although there is consensus about the importance of PSR, it is the most elusive of the four and the one frequently assigned to someone else to worry about. AAC&U commonly refers to it as "the orphan outcome." Yet Fluker (2009) notes its critical importance in our current moment in history, arguing that our nation is "struggling with a financial crisis precipitated by unscrupulous ethical practices on Wall Street" (p. vii) among other large, deeply troubling issues. To prepare students for the kind of ethical leadership in work, personal life, and civic life that Fluker describes and to raise the visibility of this outcome, AAC&U sought to provide national leadership by, among other things, launching *Core Commitments: Educating Students for Personal and Social Responsibility* in 2006, funded generously by the Templeton Foundation.

The intellectual heart of Core Commitments reflects five distinct but related dimensions of PSR. Through its robust nationwide campaign, Liberal Education and America's Promise, AAC&U has waged a highly visible public campaign to argue that personal and social responsibility are indispensable outcomes of a college education for every student. Such outcomes are needed in all parts of life and in every sphere of social endeavor. The five dimensions of PSR are research based, intended to resonate with broad constituencies inside and outside of higher education, and designed so that they can be both fostered and assessed. They include:

Striving for excellence: developing a strong work ethic and consciously doing one's very best in all aspects of college;

Cultivating personal and academic integrity: recognizing and acting on a sense of honor, ranging from honesty in relationships to principled engagement with a formal academic honor code;

Contributing to a larger community: recognizing and acting on one's responsibility to the educational community and the wider society, locally, nationally, and globally;

Taking seriously the perspectives of others: recognizing and acting on the obligation to inform one's own judgment; engaging diverse and competing perspectives as a resource for learning, citizenship, and work; and

Developing competence in ethical and moral reasoning and action: developing ethical and moral reasoning in ways that incorporate the other four responsibilities; using such reasoning in learning and in life.

In the course of the Core Commitments Initiative, AAC&U learned several important things, especially through AAC&U's Personal and Social Responsibility Inventory (PSRI), a new campus climate instrument administered at 23 Core Commitments campuses in fall 2007 by the University of Michigan under the late Eric Dey at the Center for the Study of Higher and Postsecondary Education. The PSRI is now being administered in partnership with AAC&U by the Research Institute for Studies in Education (RISE) at Iowa State University under the directorship of Robert Reason, the editor of this volume. RISE is committed to developing a national repository of data that should be of inestimable value to higher education as it tracks trends and learns more about practices that cultivate PSR.

In 2007, the PSRI showed overwhelming consensus among students and campus professionals (faculty, student affairs professionals, and academic administrators) that education for PSR *should* be a major focus of college. But, as the PSRI also showed, even highly engaged colleges and universities are not meeting this goal. Across both groups of respondents, far fewer strongly agreed that such education currently was a major focus at their institution. There was a striking gap between "should be" and "actually is" with a difference of more than 50% on some items.

In terms of support for the five dimensions of PSR found in the PSRI— striving for excellence, cultivating personal and academic integrity, contributing to a larger community, taking seriously the perspectives of others, and developing competence in ethical and moral reasoning and action—the fifth dimension lagged behind the other four in terms of endorsement by both students and campus professionals. This was true even though among the 9,000 campus professionals, only 5% strongly agreed that students possess a well-developed capacity for moral and ethical reasoning when they first enter college, and only 38% strongly agreed that students possess an increased capacity for ethical and moral reasoning at graduation compared to the beginning of college.

Adding to the conundrum, the 2007 PSRI findings indicate that to discuss questions or concerns about their own ethical and moral thinking and the challenges they face, students turn to other students more often than they turn to faculty or student affairs personnel. In fact, less than 30% of students strongly agreed that they felt they *could* turn to these educators, which suggests that seven out of 10 students are trying to navigate their own moral development without the resource of higher education's key professionals.

In terms of contributing to the larger community, PSRI data from 24,000 students and 9,000 campus professionals help explain part of the reason young people are as disengaged from civic and political involvement. Only one-third of student respondents strongly agreed that while in college their civic awareness had expanded, their civic skills enriched to help them effectively change society for the better, or their civic commitment to improve society had grown (Dey, Barnhardt, Antonaros, Ott, & Holsapple, 2009). About that same number in the 2007 PSRI survey strongly agreed that their campus actively promotes awareness of U.S. or global social, political, and economic issues. A further part of the explanation for the low percentage of growth in civic responsibility can be traced to what the students surveyed revealed about faculty attitudes and practices. Only 35.8% of college students strongly agreed that faculty publicly advocate the need for students to become active and involved citizens.

These figures dramatize the challenge before higher education if it is to respond to the National Call for Action represented in the report, *A Crucible Moment: College Learning and Democracy's Future* released at the White House in January 2012 (National Task Force on Civic Learning and Democratic Engagement, 2012). Directed by Global Perspective Inventory, Inc. and AAC&U under a contract from the U.S. Department of Education, the project organized a series of national roundtables involving 150 educators, researchers, civic organizations, policy makers, disciplinary associations, and philanthropists who shaped the report's recommendations. *A Crucible Moment* lays out an ambitious agenda for higher education and other stakeholders to take the foundational work laid thus far to scale so civic learning and democratic engagement is expected rather than optional and by design rather than by happenstance.

If higher education is to make further progress, however, some fundamental problems need to be addressed. In a survey of chief academic officers (CAOs) at AAC&U member campuses, eight out of 10 campuses reported having common learning goals for students, yet only 59% of these campuses included ethical reasoning among them, and only 53% included civic engagement among them. Furthermore, when asked if they thought students clearly understood the educational goals their institutions had set out for them, only 5% of these CAOs believed that almost all their students understood their institution's intended learning outcomes (Hart Research Associates, 2009).

In a well-known study of college students and spirituality, researchers Alexander and Helen Astin note, "About two-thirds [of today's entering college freshmen] consider it 'essential' or 'very important' that their college enhance their self-understanding (69%), prepare them for responsible citizenship (67%), develop their personal values (67%), and provide for their emotional development (63%)" (Higher Education Research Institute, 2004, p. 6). The Astins' research offers a partial explanation of one source of the discrepancy. Their findings show that a majority of students (59.7%) report that their professors never "encouraged discussions of religious/spiritual matters," and only 19.6% report that their professors "frequently encouraged exploration of questions of meaning and purpose" (Higher Education Research Institute, 2007, p. 2).

All of these findings document a sobering misalignment between aspirations, goals, and expectations, on the one hand, and students' actual educational experiences, on the other. Students come to college wanting and needing support to develop civic and moral judgments to inform their actions. But their needs are not being met. To close the gap, campuses will need to institutionalize efforts to a scale and a depth that engages all students meaningfully and over time.

Core Commitments offered an alternative framework for how higher education organizes its work. As such, it might be one that can be more widely adopted to spur further progress. Core Commitments' philosophy argued that:

• Higher education institutions have an educational and civic obligation to unapologetically teach for PSR.
• Education for PSR, to be intentionally fostered in all students, should pervade institutional cultures.
• Student learning is the collective responsibility of all individuals and units responsible for the curriculum and cocurriculum.
• Ethical, civic, and moral development should be closely tied to a substantive vision for student learning in the college years that is shared across constituent groups.
• The development of PSR is cumulative, builds on prior knowledge and experience, and should be assessed along the way.

AAC&U's clarion call to engage students with core questions about their ethical responsibilities to self and others and about their responsibilities as citizens in a diverse democracy not only struck a resounding chord but revealed a burgeoning movement.

AAC&U has not been alone in fostering leadership in this arena. Throughout Core Commitments and now in the national coalition that is working together to promote the goals of *A Crucible Moment*, the National Association of Student Personnel Administrators (NASPA) has exerted consistent leadership foregrounding the importance of PSR through publications, projects, and national conferences. Since *A Crucible Moment* was released, it has been heartening to be part of a national action task force, convened by AAC&U, that has been working in concert with other organizations and foundations to coordinate, strategize, and amplify efforts to make education for PSR woven into the fabric of higher education. In addition to NASPA and AAC&U, the National Action Task Force for *A Crucible Moment* includes national organizations and foundations that have been leading the way: the Anchors Task Force, the Association of American State Colleges and Universities, the Bonner Foundation, Bringing Theory to Practice, Campus Compact, the Center for Information & Research on Civic Learning and Engagement at Tufts University, the Democracy Commitment: A Community College Initiative, Imagining America, the Interfaith Youth Core, the Kettering Foundation, and New England Resource Center for Higher Education. This ever-increasing and collaborative groundswell of leadership promises to alter how college students are educated for generations to come.

The directions higher education needs to go are clearer than ever as this volume reveals. It is critical to implement and assess carefully thought out, integrated programs, practices, and pedagogies that promote PSR as an expected outcome of every student's college education. Such explicit, deliberate, and pervasive actions can help students acquire new ethical and civic capacities by design rather than by chance.

It was heartening to read the results of the 2007–08 Higher Education Research Institute Faculty Survey, which reflect the views of 22,562 full-time college faculty at 372 4-year colleges and universities. In the 3 years since the last polling, there has been a significant shift in faculty goals for undergraduate education in terms of receptiveness to PSR goals. The percentage of faculty saying it is "very important" or "essential" that faculty should help students develop moral character has jumped from 57.1% to 70.2%. There is an even greater percentage shift in support for helping students develop personal values—from 50.8% to 66.1%. Similarly, the percentage of support for instilling a commitment to community service has leapt from 36.4% to 55.5% (DeAngelo, Hurtado, Pryor, Santos, & Korn, 2009, p. 3).

What AAC&U found in its evaluation of what mattered most to Core Commitments participating institutions suggests directions for the next generation of PSR work more generally. These findings are echoed throughout many of the articles in this volume:

- foster a shared language about institutional values and educational goals for students;
- tighten and formalize cross-campus leadership and coordination, particularly across academic affairs and student affairs and across different disciplines;
- legitimize the importance of education for PSR;
- identify gaps between what is valued and what is actually practiced;

- identify areas of innovations and share resources; and
- quicken progress on reaching important but as-yet-unrealized goals.

By following these guideposts, higher education might bring Jonathan Kozol's quest to fruition: "an entire ethos of ethical responsibility for the nation's greater good ... ought to be pervasive in the atmosphere of learning at every college and university in this land" (as cited in Carlson, 2009, "A Question for the President," para. 4).

References

Association of American Colleges and Universities (AAC&U). (2007). *College learning for the new global century: A report from the National Leadership Council for Liberal Education & America's Promise.* Washington, DC: Author.

Carlson, S. (2009, July 21). College planners hear lament for liberal arts and public schools. *Chronicle of Higher Education.* Retrieved from https://chronicle.com/article/College-Planners-Hear-Lament/117567/

DeAngelo, L., Hurtado, S., Pryor, J., Santos, J., & Korn, W. (2009). *The American college teacher: National norms for the faculty 2007–2008 HERI Faculty Survey.* Los Angeles: University of California, Los Angeles.

Dey, E. L., Barnhardt, C. L., Antonaros, M., Ott, M. C., & Holsapple, M. A. (2009). *Civic responsibility: What is the campus climate for learning?* Washington, DC: Association of American Colleges and Universities.

Fluker, W. E. (2009). *Ethical leadership: The quest for character, civility, and community.* Minneapolis, MN: Fortress Press.

Hart Research Associates. (2009). *Learning and assessment: Trends in undergraduate education (A survey among members of the Association of American Colleges and Universities).* Washington, DC: Association of American Colleges and Universities. Retrieved from www.aacu.org/membership/documents/2009MemberSurvey_Part1.pdf

Higher Education Research Institute. (2004). *The spiritual life of college students: A national study of college students' search for meaning and purpose.* Los Angeles: Higher Education Research Institute at University of California, Los Angeles. Retrieved from http://spirituality.ucla.edu/docs/reports/Spiritual_Life_College_Students_Full_Report.pdf

Higher Education Research Institute. (2007, December 18). *Additional information on First Longitudinal Study of Students' Spiritual Growth* [News release]. Los Angeles: Higher Education Research Institute at University of California, Los Angeles. Retrieved from http://spirituality.ucla.edu/docs/news/report_backup_dec07 release_12.18.07.pdf

National Task Force on Civic Learning and Democratic Engagement. (2012). *A crucible moment: College learning and democracy's future.* Washington, DC: Association of American Colleges and Universities.

CARYN MCTIGHE MUSIL *is a senior scholar and director of Civic Learning and Democracy Initiatives at the Association of American Colleges and Universities.*

2

This chapter examines the existing literature in two major areas. A review of literature related to higher education's mission to educate for personal and social responsibility provides a rationale to refocus our collective attention on this important area of student learning and development. The chapter also reviews the current understanding on how well colleges and universities are currently doing in educating for personal and social responsibility.

Higher Education's Role in Educating for Personal and Social Responsibility: A Review of Existing Literature

Robert D. Reason, Andrew J. Ryder, Chad Kee

What kind of people do we want our children and grandchildren to be? What kind of society do we want them to live in? How can we best shape our institutions to nurture those kinds of people and that kind of society?

Kezar, Chambers, & Burkhardt, 2005, p. 324

Educating students for personal and social responsibility (PSR) has roots in American higher education history. The priority placed on educating for PSR in higher education has waxed and waned over time (Checkoway, 2000), assuming primacy during the early years of higher education in the United States then losing favor until the recent resurgence (Checkoway, 2000; Rudolph, 1962). Strong components of educating for PSR existed during the early establishment of higher education institutions through the promotion of civic engagement, engagement in community service, serving the public good, and volunteering (Rudolph, 1962). Faculty members emphasized intellectual development of college students, to the detriment of other forms of development, during the late 1800s and early 1900s. Although some attention was paid to civic engagement during the early to mid-1900s, in particular with Dewey's emphasis on engaged education in the 1920s and 1930s, intellectual development remained, and remains, the primary emphasis of higher education. Educating for PSR, as part of a holistic understanding of student learning, is making a resurgence currently, likely due to the work of the Association of American Colleges &

NEW DIRECTIONS FOR HIGHER EDUCATION, no. 164, Winter 2013 © Wiley Periodicals, Inc.
Published online in Wiley Online Library (wileyonlinelibrary.com) • DOI:10.1002/he.20072

Universities (AAC&U), the Obama Administration's emphasis on civic education, and recent higher education research studying the effects of service learning and volunteerism. It is important to acknowledge that large bodies of literature exist that offer related practices of service learning and civic engagement.

Recent literature reveals a disconnection between the ideals of educating students for PSR and the actual practice on college campuses (Dey & Associates, 2009, 2010a, 2010b). Fortunately, scholars and practitioners are beginning to address the need to bridge the theoretical and practical to create campus communities that intentionally educate for PSR. AAC&U (2010) has taken a leadership role in advancing the research and practice through the Core Commitments Initiative. This initiative brings the conversation of PSR to the forefront of higher education research and practice. AAC&U's focus on educating for PSR is intended to strengthen the capacity to engage college students in thoughtful and effective dialogue and learning opportunities.

The purpose of this chapter is to examine the current arguments relevant to educating students for PSR. In addition, the aim of this chapter is to identify implications for future research. To offer a comprehensive approach, the chapter addresses three broad areas: why educate for PSR, what are the challenges encountered on college campuses that impede PSR education, and what do we know currently about how college affects students' development of PSR. The existing literature generally does not use the language of PSR or the five dimensions identified by AAC&U's (2010) Core Commitments Initiative. We do, however, present the brief literature review of PSR outcomes, using AAC&U's five dimensions as a framework. Because later chapters in this volume highlight effective educational practices, including those arising directly from the Core Commitments Initiative, this literature review focuses more generally on PSR outcomes.

Why Educate for Personal and Social Responsibility?

Caryn McTighe Musil, in Chapter 1 of this volume, lays out the justification for reemphasizing education for PSR in higher education, including the importance of preparing students for effective participation in civic life; raising awareness of societal problems among campus community; and strengthening undergraduate education in search of solutions to those problems. Gutmann (1987), Hamrick (1998), Hurtado (2007), and Reason (2011) have all argued that higher education institutions have a civic mission. Preparing active citizens willing to engage in community life and able to effectively communicate across demographic, ideological, and political differences is an essential component of higher education's civic mission.

Current events within the larger society such as concerns about leadership of financial, political, and social institutions; ideological and demographic trends creating a society that is increasingly diverse in myriad ways; the lingering economic recession; and persistent inequities within educational structures illuminate the need to provide intentional learning opportunities that support civic and moral development among students. O'Neill (2012) argued the need to educate for PSR can easily be affirmed through examination of the workings of Wall Street: "One need only to look at recent troubling Wall Street practices to realize the necessity in having a sense of ethics and social responsibility and an ability to think critically to accompany a deep knowledge of business that many students hope to gain in college" (p. 2). Checkoway (2011) concluded that the continued movement toward a more multicultural population in the United States will demand that students be aware of their own identities, capable of communicating across differences, and possess the skills necessary to develop positive relationships across cultures. Higher education must focus on helping students to become informed citizens capable of addressing social issues justly in a multicultural society.

The National Task Force on Civic Learning and Democratic Engagement called on higher education to take action to combat what they called "civic malaise" (2012, p. 6). The evidence of this malaise can be seen in low voter turnout, poor demonstration of knowledge on civics tests, and moribund high school civics curriculum requirements. Fewer high school seniors in 2010 scored as proficient or advanced in civics knowledge than scored below the basic level, for example (National Center for Education Statistics, 2010). Students are coming to higher education unprepared to engage in their civic responsibilities, a situation that colleges and universities must not leave unaddressed.

Higher education institutions must not focus only on social responsibility, in the form of civic participation; we must attend to the development of personal responsibility as well. AAC&U's Core Commitments Initiative uses the language of excellence, integrity, and moral and ethical reasoning to describe personal responsibility (Dey & Associates, 2010a); later in this volume Carol Trosset (Chapter 3) encourages us to take an ever broader view of personal responsibility to include responsibility to work and family, presenting evidence of behavioral concerns among college students that point to limited development of personal responsibility. Concerns about academic dishonesty, abuse of alcohol, and violence against other students certainly reinforce the need to focus on personal responsibility on campus.

Finally, a compelling reason for educating students for PSR is that both students and campus professionals believe this is an essential outcome of college (Dey & Associates, 2009). Fully 90% of both students and campus professionals surveyed by Dey and his colleagues agreed that PSR *should be* a major focus of higher education. Over half of all students *strongly agreed* with this statement. This finding indicates a recognized demand for education that prepares students to actively engage as citizens.

What Are the Challenges of Educating Students to Become Personally and Socially Responsible?

The arguments in favor of educating for PSR notwithstanding, educators encounter persistent and potentially intractable challenges to implementing interventions aimed at developing PSR. Three significant challenges emerged from the literature: (a) higher education has deemphasized its historical mission promoting civic engagement and participation, (b) faculty members are unable to clearly define their role in educating for PSR, and (c) students are less likely to be involved in learning opportunities that encourage PSR as they move through their undergraduate education.

Deemphasizing Personal and Social Responsibility. In his classic history of American higher education, Rudolph (1962) reasoned that character development exceeded intellectual development during the early years of colleges and universities. If we understand PSR to be part of character development for students, then we can trace the development of PSR back to the original purpose and mission of American higher education. Checkoway (2001a) supported Rudolph's claim by suggesting that American universities were guided by a civic mission to prepare students to operate effectively within a diverse democracy.

We would argue, however, that PSR is not a central emphasis of higher education today. Colby and Sullivan (2009) referred to these outcomes as "distantly connected" and a "by-product" of postsecondary education (p. 29). Educating students for PSR has taken a back seat to intellectual development and, in some cases, skill development and job training. PSR is often understood as the product of informal learning that is best left to students' personal initiative or those campus professionals focused on out-of-class activities. The transition toward greater institutional emphasis on content knowledge acquisition may be attributed to the evolution of universities and colleges becoming more like businesses and adopting business techniques, requiring institutions to compete with other institutions (Seguine, 2000). The newfound emphasis on institutional competition further relegates the development of PSR in students.

Faculty Role in Educating for Personal and Social Responsibility. A well-developed empirical research base establishes faculty members as the primary socialization agents in higher education, sending explicit and implicit messages about what is important in academic communities (Pascarella & Terenzini, 2005). Unfortunately, faculty members may be unable to define their role as educators for PSR (Checkoway, 2001b). Faculty uncertainty may be a product of pressures to produce grants, research, and publications crowding out classroom instruction and development of PSR as part of their jobs. Checkoway (2001b) explained the challenges faced when attempting to engage faculty in the role of educating for PSR:

> There are serious obstacles to involving faculty in renewing the civic mission of the research university. First, faculty [members] do not always perceive

themselves or their professional roles in this way; indeed, they are conditioned to believe that the civic competencies of students and the problems of society are not central to their roles in the university. They view themselves as teachers and researchers with commitments to their academic disciplines or professional fields, but this does not necessarily translate into playing public roles in an engaged university or democratic society. (p. 135)

Faculty scholarly productivity is important, but its overemphasis at certain institutions threatens the democratic mission of higher education in the United States.

The ambiguity concerning faculty roles and responsibilities in educating for PSR may negatively influence students' involvement in civic learning opportunities. It is safe to assume that faculty members who are unsure of their roles as educators of PSR may deemphasize or avoid learning opportunities that promote dialogue related to politics, economics, religion, or race relations. Consequently, students may not be encouraged to participate in those learning opportunities that enhance their PSR competencies.

Decreasing Student Involvement in Personal and Social Responsibility. As students move beyond their first year, they may become consumed with personal areas of interests such as social networks, employment, and graduation and grow less engaged in experiential learning (Checkoway, 2001a). Reason, Terenzini, and Domingo (2007) found that students' involvement in public participation is shaped by their precollege experiences that predispose them to engage with learning opportunities that may enhance their PSR. Unfortunately, the influence of precollege experiences appears to wane, as demonstrated by the general decrease in civic engagement over the 4 years of students' college careers (Dey & Associates, 2009).

Research findings arising from the Personal and Social Responsibility Inventory (PSRI) suggest the institutional emphasis on PSR decreases with each successive year in higher education (Dey & Associates, 2009, 2010a, 2010b). Whether students become less involved, and therefore perceive less institutional emphasis, or less institutional emphasis results in less student involvement, is not known; but the combination of decreased involvement and decreased perceptions of institutional emphasis creates an environment in which the development of PSR is difficult to maintain over time.

Personal and Social Responsibility Outcomes

We know from existing literature that college experiences affect the development of outcomes related to PSR (Pascarella & Terenzini, 2005). Although most researchers are not using the specific language used in this volume, or by AAC&U in the development of their Core Commitments Initiative, a solid empirical literature base exists. In an effort to connect the existing literature to the Core Commitments Initiative, we employ the five dimensions of PSR as an organizing framework for this section.

Students Learn to Strive for Excellence. AAC&U described striving for excellence as the pursuit of a strong work ethic and consciously doing one's very best in all aspects of college life. O'Neill (2012) operationalized this dimension to include the Habits of Mind for Lifelong Learning scale from Higher Education Research Institute (HERI) and scales related to academic motivation and need for cognition that are being used in the Wabash National Study of Liberal Arts Education (WNSLAE). These three scales are related to each other in that each assesses students' efforts to learn and enjoyment of engaging with new information.

Unfortunately, according to O'Neill's (2012) review of the empirical research related to these outcomes, students generally demonstrate limited gains—and often experience losses—on these scales in college. Interestingly, students responding to the PSRI, the instrument developed through the Core Commitments Initiative, reported that experiences during college assisted them in increasing their work ethic. It appears from these data that students' experiences and self-reported gains are at odds.

Students Learn to Cultivate Academic Integrity. Recognizing and acting on a sense of honor, ranging from honesty in relationships to principled engagement with a formal academic honors code is AAC&U's definition of academic integrity. Academic integrity is most easily operationalized as not cheating on academic assignments, but the assessment of this dimension on the PSRI also includes items related to plagiarism and improper citation.

Although estimates of the prevalence of cheating among college students differ widely, the majority of studies indicate that over half of all college students admit to cheating while in college. In a comprehensive study of well over 50,000 college students, the Center for Academic Integrity (McCabe, 2005) estimated that about 70% of all students admit to cheating on an exam and approximately 50% admit to cheating on a paper. Prevalent forms of cheating also included using unpermitted notes on a take-home exam, copying short passages without citation, and asking other students about exam questions and content.

Students Learn to Contribute to a Larger Community. Contributing to a larger community involves recognizing and acting upon one's responsibility for the general welfare of others in the larger community—within and beyond the college campus. O'Neill's (2012) review of empirical research related existing evidence about social agency, civic awareness, socially responsible leadership, and political and social involvement to this dimension. The Core Commitments Initiative and the PSRI include awareness of U.S. and global social, political, and economic issues in the understanding of contributing to the larger community. The importance of community and civic action has received a great deal of attention, especially since the release of *A Crucible Moment* in January 2012 (National Task Force on Civic Learning and Democratic Engagement, 2012).

Community and civic action takes many forms. Often the simplest forms of engagement serve as the most prevalent indicators of community and civic action. Research on voting and volunteering, two forms of community engagement, indicates that citizens with bachelor's degrees or higher are more likely to do both. Pascarella and Terenzini (2005) estimated, for example, that individuals with at least a bachelor's degree are "perhaps 30 percentage points more likely than those with no postsecondary education to volunteer for a community service group" (p. 278).

The positive effect of college is less clear when we switch the focus from civic *action* to civic *learning*. Civic learning outcomes include the knowledge, skills, and values necessary to understand and navigate the complex processes of a democratic society (National Task Force on Civic Learning and Democratic Engagement, 2012). Evidence of the current state of "civic malaise" (p. 6) noted earlier in this chapter, highlights the limited civic learning that occurs during college.

Students Learn to Take Seriously the Perspectives of Others. Taking seriously the perspectives of others is recognizing and acting on the obligation to inform one's own judgment. This dimension of PSR also includes engaging diverse and competing perspectives as a resource for learning, citizenship, and work. Dey and colleagues (2010b) identified a series of attitudes and values from existing literature that related directly to this dimension, including:

- respect for differing viewpoints;
- the ability to thoroughly gather evidence to support ideas;
- the capacity to consider diverse perspectives;
- the potential to reconsider one's own perspective; and
- the ability to explore diverse perspectives, cultures, and worldviews. (p. 2)

O'Neill (2012) added to this comprehensive list by linking findings from existing studies of pluralistic orientation, the Miville-Guzman Universality-Diversity Scale, and openness to diversity and challenge.

The relationship between college attendance and openness to diverse perspectives is well established in the research of higher education (Pascarella & Terenzini, 2005). So too is the importance of this area of outcome. Hurtado (2007) linked development of perspective taking directly to the development of citizen leaders: "This emerging work on the educational benefits of diversity is part of a long-term effort to transform undergraduate education which will prepare the next generation of citizens for a multicultural society" (p. 186).

Research related to the Core Commitments Initiative reinforces the conclusion that students gain in this dimension during college (O'Neill,

2012). Students' self-reported gains from the PSRI grow consistently over time during college (Dey & Associates, 2010b). Unfortunately, an evaluation of results from both HERI and WNSLAE surveys led O'Neill (2012) to conclude that "overall gains across students are often modest, and in many instances, the gains made by some students were, in effect, 'cancelled out' by a lack of gains or even losses among other students" (p. 27). This finding makes intuitive sense, even as it is disappointing to educators who hope to develop perspective taking in college students. Certainly the review of diversity-related outcomes research completed by Pascarella and Terenzini (2005) underscores the importance of *engaging* with diverse others and ideas in the development of such outcomes.

Students Learn to Develop Competence in Ethical and Moral Reasoning and Action. The final dimension defined by AAC&U is developing ethical and moral reasoning and action, which suggests that students should incorporate the other four dimensions into their ethical and moral reasoning and use that reasoning in learning and in life. The PSRI operationalizes this dimension as students' ability to express and act upon their values (Dey & Associates, 2010a).

Much of the research related to college students' development of ethical and moral reasoning in college draws upon Kohlberg's (1984) theoretical framework as a guide, often using Rest's (1986) Defining Issues Test as an instrument to collect data (King & Mayhew, 2005; Pascarella & Terenzini, 2005). In reviewing many of these studies, Pascarella and Terenzini (2005) concluded that "the college experience itself has a unique and positive influence on increases in principled moral reasoning" (p. 347). These authors also conclude that growth in moral reasoning *should* result in more principled action by students, although they readily admit that the empirical link between moral reasoning and action is, at best, mixed.

Conclusion

Although the findings are mixed, the literature reviewed (e.g., Pascarella & Terenzini, 2005) suggests that attending college generally has a positive effect on the development of outcomes related to PSR. The influence of college on these outcomes is related both to specific interventions like service learning and a general sense of climate created on campus. The following chapters in this volume focus specifically on the study of climate for the development of PSR and on some policies and practices implemented by institutions that participated in the Core Commitments Initiative.

Education for engaged citizenship has been an essential mission of higher education from its origins as colonial colleges (Rudolph, 1962), although some have argued that we have deemphasized that mission in favor of knowledge generation and dissemination (Checkoway, 2000; National Task Force on Civic Learning and Democratic Engagement, 2012). Certainly contemporary political, economic, and environmental issues call for educated and civil engagement across differences (O'Neill, 2012). This volume, and AAC&U's Core Commitments Initiative, serves as a call to refocus our efforts on the development of personally and socially responsible citizens.

References

Association of American Colleges and Universities. (2010). *Core commitments: Educating students for personal and social responsibility*. Retrieved from http://www.aacu.org/core_commitments/index.cfm

Checkoway, B. (2000). Public service: Our new mission. *Academe, 86*, 24–28.

Checkoway, B. (2001a). Renewing the civic mission of the American research university. *The Journal of Higher Education, 72*(2), 125–147.

Checkoway, B. (2001b). Strategies for involving faculty in civic renewal. *Journal of College and Character, 2*(5), 1–22.

Checkoway, B. (2011). What is youth participation? *Children and Youth Services Review, 33*(2), 340–345.

Colby, A., & Sullivan, W. M. (2009). Strengthening the foundation of students' excellence, integrity, and social contribution. *Liberal Education, 95*, 22–30.

Dey, E. L., & Associates. (2009). *Civic responsibility: What is the campus climate for learning?* Washington, DC: Association of American Colleges and Universities.

Dey, E. L., & Associates. (2010a). *Developing a moral compass: What is the campus climate for ethics and academic integrity?* Washington, DC: Association of American Colleges and Universities.

Dey, E. L., & Associates. (2010b). *Engaging diverse viewpoints: What is the campus climate for perspective taking?* Washington, DC: Association of American Colleges and Universities.

Gutmann, A. (1987). Unity and diversity in democratic multcultural education: Creative and destructive tensions. In J. A. Banks (Ed.), *Diversity and citizenship education: Global perspectives* (pp. 71–98). San Francisco, CA: Jossey-Bass.

Hamrick, F. A. (1998). Democratic citizenship and student activism. *Journal of College Student Development, 39*(5), 449–459.

Hurtado, S. (2007). Linking diversity with the educational and civic missions of higher education. *The Review of Higher Education, 30*(2), 185–196.

Kezar, A. J., Chambers, T. C., & Burkhardt, J. (2005). *Higher education for the public good: Emerging voices from a national movement*. San Francisco, CA: Jossey-Bass.

King, P. M., & Mayhew, M. J. (2005). Theory and research on the development of moral reasoning among college students. In J. C. Smart (Ed.), *Higher education: Handbook of theory and research* (Vol. 19, pp. 375–440). Dordrecht, The Netherlands: Kluwer Academic.

Kohlberg, L. (1984). *Essays on moral development: The psychology of moral development* (Vol. 2). San Francisco, CA: HarperCollins.

McCabe, D. (2005). Levels of cheating and plagiarism remain high. *CAI Research*. Durham, NC: Center for Academic Integrity, Duke University.

National Center for Education Statistics. (2010). *The nation's report card: Civics 2010*. Washington, DC: Institute of Education Sciences, U.S. Department of Education.

National Task Force on Civic Learning and Democratic Engagement. (2012). *A crucible moment: College learning and democracy's future*. Washington, DC: Association of American Colleges and Universities.

O'Neill, N. (2012). *Promising practices for personal and social responsibility: Findings from a national research collaborative*. Washington, DC: Association of American Colleges and Universities.

Pascarella, E. T., & Terenzini, P. T. (2005). *How college affects students. Vol. 2: A third decade of research*. San Francisco, CA: Jossey-Bass.

Reason, R. D. (2011). Expanding the conversation. Perspective taking as a civic outcome of college. *Journal of College and Character, 12*(2). doi:10.2202/1940-1639.1786

Reason, R. D., Terenzini, P. T., & Domingo, R. J. (2007). Developing social and personal competence in the first year of college. *The Review of Higher Education, 30*(3), 271–299.

Rest, J. R. (1986). *Moral development: Advances in research and theory*. New York, NY: Praeger.

Rudolph, F. (1962). *The American college and university: A history*. New York, NY: Vintage Books.

Seguine, J. (2000). Education alumni discuss higher ed challenges, future perspectives. *The University Record*. Retrieved from http://ur.umich.edu/0001/Oct16_00/8.htm

ROBERT D. REASON *is associate professor of higher education at Iowa State University and director of the Personal and Social Responsibility Inventory.*

ANDREW J. RYDER *is assistant professor of higher education at the University of North Carolina, Wilmington. He previously served as project director for the Personal and Social Responsibility Inventory at Iowa State University.*

CHAD KEE *is performance accountability coordinator at the Office of the State Superintendent of Education in Washington, DC. He previously served as a graduate assistant for the Personal and Social Responsibility Inventory at Iowa State University.*

3

Higher education literature has focused narrowly on social responsibility to the exclusion of personal responsibility. This chapter challenges higher education researchers and practitioners to include behaviors related to personal responsibility in their research and educational agendas.

Broadening Our Understanding and Assessment of Personal and Social Responsibility: A Challenge to Researchers and Practitioners

Carol Trosset

Despite the Association of American Colleges and Universities' (AAC&U) broad definition of responsibility in the Core Commitments Initiative, recent discourse on the subject has focused on whether students hold certain social justice values or participate in service learning or other forms of civic engagement. Research abounds on these types of social responsibility; however, responsibility is not just about valuing social justice. The limited research literature on personal responsibility tends to focus on cheating and plagiarism, leaving such issues as academic commitment or personal obligations to job and family relatively unstudied. In this chapter I explore the need for both researchers and campus leaders to adopt a broader understanding of the concept of responsibility, to focus less on values and more on student behavior and its outcomes.

Exploring Student Values

To explore a range of student values and behaviors related to responsibility, I examined a large data set including 5 years of student survey data from the Cooperative Institutional Research Program (CIRP) freshman survey and the National Survey of Student Engagement (NSSE), representing 123 private institutions between 2006–07 and 2010–11, and Wabash National Study data from four of these institutions, including fall 2006 data on

NEW DIRECTIONS FOR HIGHER EDUCATION, no. 164, Winter 2013 © Wiley Periodicals, Inc.
Published online in Wiley Online Library (wileyonlinelibrary.com) • DOI:10.1002/he.20073

entering first-year students and spring 2007 and spring 2010 data on the same students' experiences and characteristics.[1]

Most of the questions from these surveys that relate to responsibility ask about students' life goals, which can be considered a measure of their values. Many of these address typical dimensions of civic engagement, such as how important it is to students that they become community leaders or promote racial harmony. Other items ask about different ways of being responsible for something, like the importance of raising a family or running one's own business.

To determine whether all kinds of responsibility are valued by the same students, I performed a factor analysis of all the CIRP questions asking about goals or behaviors related to issues of personal or social responsibility. Factor analysis is a statistical technique that identifies sets of questions to which people tend to give similar responses. If a group of questions belongs to a single factor, that means that many people who gave a high score in answer to one of them also gave high scores to the others. Such a pattern shows that this group of questions is probably measuring a single unifying concept. My analysis showed that students tend to answer these questions as if they described two distinct sets of values, which are referred to here as "social responsibility" and "personal responsibility." Table 3.1 shows which questions formed each of the two factors.

Two factor scores were calculated for each individual survey respondent, one for the importance he or she assigned to social responsibility goals and another for personal responsibility. For individual students, the two sets of goals are unrelated; a given student might care about one but not the other, or about both, or neither. Note that students with low scores may have strong but very focused values and goals. For example, a student might be very concerned about the environment but not want to pursue the political side of those concerns. Another might be very committed to becoming an authority in theoretical mathematics and be genuinely uninterested in every other goal listed on the survey. For college leaders attempting to promote a particular version of responsibility, it is important to remember that things like civic engagement are not just natural human values already shared by everyone at the institution. Likewise, they should not assume that students who arrive at college without a strong concern for social responsibility issues are disengaged or adrift.

Average scores were then calculated for each institution. These scores were used to characterize the culture of responsibility at each institution, based on the prevailing values of the incoming students. When comparing institution-level scores, social and personal responsibility values are negatively correlated. That is, at most institutions in this data set, the student

---

[1]Thanks to the Higher Education Data Sharing Consortium for their permission to use these data for this analysis.

Table 3.1. CIRP Questions Related to Social and Personal Responsibility

	Social Responsibility	Personal Responsibility
Important Goals	Participate in community action	Become an authority in my field
	Help to promote racial harmony	Become successful in a business of my own
	Improve my understanding of other countries and cultures	Have administrative responsibility for the work of others
	Become a community leader	Raise a family
	Keep up to date with political affairs	
	Influence the political structure	
	Influence social values	
	Help others who are in difficulty	
	Become involved in programs to clean up the environment	
	Adopt green practices to protect the environment	
Likely Future Actions	Participate in volunteer or community service work	
	Participate in student protests or demonstrations	
	Participate in student clubs or groups	

body on average places a high value on one set of goals and a low value on the other. Students at 40 of these 123 institutions placed a high value on social responsibility and a low value on personal responsibility (let's call this Type 1); students at another 40 institutions placed a high value on personal responsibility and a low value on social responsibility (Type 2). Most of the remaining 43 student cultures placed either a moderate or a low average value on both types, whereas a few valued both highly.

What does it mean for an institution to have a dominant set of social values? I examined four colleges participating in the Wabash National Study, two of which placed a high average value on social responsibility and a low average value on personal responsibility (Type 1), and two with the opposite profile (Type 2). At each of these institutions, only about 30% of the individual students held that same set of values. Five to 10% held the opposite value profile, whereas a clear majority of 60–65% did not fit either profile and valued both sets of goals about equally. Based on my own involvement with some of these institutions, the dominant value set is something most people on campus are clearly aware of, and there is a tendency for some members of the institution to assume that everyone shares those values. Clearly, however, the high-social or high-personal responsibility value sets are hegemonic rather than universal; that is, they become part of the common discourse in a way that is hard to ignore or avoid, whether or not an individual agrees with them.

The social responsibility values listed in these surveys mostly support the Core Commitments dimension of "contributing to the larger community" (see http://www.psri.hs.iastate.edu/dimensions.php for a full description of all five Core Commitments dimensions). A few—understanding other countries and cultures, and promoting racial harmony—support the "taking seriously the perspectives of others" dimension. Papers presented at the 2011 AAC&U Conference "Educating for Personal and Social Responsibility" overwhelmingly focused on the first set of values: social justice, civic engagement, and volunteer work. However, the items under "personal responsibility" also support various Core Commitments. Raising a family, running a successful business, and taking on administrative responsibility are all ways of contributing to a larger community. Becoming an authority in one's field is an important part of striving for excellence. After all, the adult world does not break down into some people who care about social causes and other people who raise families and hold administrative jobs. Many individuals who, as students, professed a desire to help others in difficulty and influence social values grow up to have families and be authorities in their fields or own their own businesses. Yet so far, the higher education community has shown less interest in documenting and assessing those values that focus on more personal types of responsibility.

Institutions with the two different value profiles differ from each other in other ways as well. Type 1 institutions, those in which students report valuing social over personal responsibility, tend to be more selective, have higher average SAT scores, and have fewer students receiving financial aid. If we look at what type of individual students have these value profiles, we find that Type 1 students are, on average, more politically liberal and less likely to be religious, and that their parents have attained higher levels of education. These patterns begin to suggest that socioeconomic status may play a role in whether individual students place more emphasis on goals like "influencing social values" or on goals like "taking administrative responsibility for the work of others." Student survey data show that economic factors play an even bigger role in students' behavior and how they spend their time while in college.

How Are Values Related to Behavior?

Whereas the CIRP survey collects data on students' values, NSSE asks students about their behavior. A number of the behaviors documented are relevant to issues of responsibility. A factor analysis of these questions revealed three main types of student behaviors: academic commitment (spending many hours preparing for class, writing multiple paper drafts, working hard to meet faculty expectations, and completing assignments on time), off-campus obligations (time spent caring for dependents, commuting to class, and working for pay off campus), and cocurricular involvement (time spent in cocurricular activities and exercising). Time spent on community service or volunteer work was, for some groups, positively associated with cocurricular involvement, but it was sometimes unrelated to all other pursuits.

Students with more off-campus obligations spent less time on cocurricular activities and were less likely to volunteer or do community service. Any definition of social responsibility that focuses too closely on community service would discount that these students are already carrying more "adult responsibilities" (a job, family) than the typical traditional-age student at a private residential college. Furthermore, Type 2 colleges (those whose students place more value on personal responsibility than on social responsibility) have more students with more off-campus obligations.

Even within the realm of civic engagement, behavior is not always congruent with values. One might expect that students who express their personal commitment to social justice life goals would be more likely than those with other values to devote their time to community service and volunteer work. In fact, this is only true of students who attend Type 1 colleges (where social service values predominate). At these institutions, about 80% of students who privilege social responsibility goals report doing community service, compared to about 40% of students for whom personal responsibility goals are more important. On the other hand, at Type 2 colleges (where personal responsibility values are dominant), almost 90% of all students perform community service, regardless of their individual values profiles.

Moreover, academic commitment—that is, behaving as a serious, responsible, student—definitely does not correlate with social justice values. Students with both value profiles reported about the same amount of time studying and were equally likely to say they worked hard in their classes. For first-year students, this was true regardless of which type of values dominated at the students' institution. Seniors attending Type 2 institutions reported greater academic commitment, regardless of which values they espoused as individuals. Admittedly, we need more data than we currently have on the relationship between students' values and their behavior. However, it is clear even from this limited evidence that values should not be used as a proxy for behavior.

Data from the first cohort of students to complete the Wabash National Study suggest that values related to social and personal responsibility do not change much during 4 years of college. The Wabash Center of Inquiry report titled "Summary of Four-Year Change" (www.liberalarts.wabash.edu /storage/4-year-change-summary-website.pdf) shows that the average score on the Political and Social Involvement scale (which contains many of the same questions as the social responsibility factor discussed in this chapter) actually goes down over 4 years in college. The same report states that although 35% of students displayed moderate to high growth on this measure, 58% experienced either no growth or a decline in this area. My own analysis of institutions with different value profiles showed that even in cases in which an individual student attended a college dominated by a different set of values, the importance assigned to both social and personal responsibility were, on average, unchanged over time.

Are values what we, as educators, are trying to cultivate? If so, we need to be careful about claiming them as outcomes, when most students may be arriving at our institutions with their social values largely intact.

The Outcomes of Responsibility

AAC&U's statements about the Core Commitments Initiative make it clear that their goal is not simply to cultivate certain values among college students, or to foster a particular type of campus climate, but to encourage various forms of responsible behavior. These behaviors include not only civic engagement but also striving for academic excellence and behaving with integrity as a member of a campus community, with respect to such things as substance abuse and social relationships with other students.

Behavior is harder to measure than values, and we usually must rely on student self-reports. For full-time undergraduates, being a student is their full-time job, so it seems appropriate to examine how responsibly they are filling that role. Unfortunately, various studies have documented a lack of responsible behavior on the part of a great many students. In *Academically Adrift*, Arum and Roksa (2011) report that in the aggregate, the 2,322 students in their study sample spent only one-fifth of their time on academic pursuits, including attending classes. The average student spent 12 hours per week doing academic work outside of class, and 37% of the sample spent less than 5 hours per week studying.

National results for 2006–2008 from the Core Institute Alcohol and Drug Survey (http://core.siu.edu/pdfs/report0608.pdf), comprising nearly 210,000 respondents, show that 66% of underage students drank alcohol within the month prior to taking the survey, and 46% of all respondents reported binge drinking sometime in the previous 2 weeks. At least 30% reported using some kind of illegal drug during that academic year. About 37% admitted to public misconduct; 36% said they did something they later regretted; and 28% reported missing class, as a result of alcohol or drug use.

Taking seriously the perspectives of others is also a behavior, and it is difficult to measure. Many students say they value diversity and also report spending time having discussions with people whose views or backgrounds are different from their own. However, discussions come in many forms, and not all involve serious consideration of other points of view. In my own research (Trosset, 1998) on the obstacles students experience when discussing diversity issues, I found that most students who liked discussing diversity issues saw these interactions as occasions for airing views they already held. Very few said anything to indicate that they wanted to learn how others might think differently. One outcome of taking other perspectives seriously should be that once in a while, one genuinely changes one's mind about something of importance. It may not be easy for students to report accurately on surveys whether or not they have done this.

There is also an academic component to taking other views seriously. Within an intellectual context, this behavior should include things like studying more than one theoretical perspective within the social sciences, and taking courses in subjects that one does not yet know much about. Residential life is another relevant domain; living fairly quietly and neatly in a dormitory can also be seen as a desired outcome of taking other people's perspectives seriously.

The Defining Issues Test, which forms part of the Wabash National Study, measures students' moral reasoning styles by asking them how they would approach various hypothetical dilemmas. Results from the first cohort of study participants show that on average, the moral reasoning style of students becomes more sophisticated during the 4 years of college. However, we have essentially no information about how students think about moral problems that arise in their own lives or how they act in response to those problems. It may or may not be possible to collect such data, but we should be cautious about assuming that anyone takes the same approach to immediate personal challenges as he or she does when considering hypothetical cases in which he or she is not involved.

What does "responsible" really mean? Dictionary definitions overwhelmingly refer to a responsible person as one who will be held to account for something by others. One is not simply "responsible"; one is responsible for something. As Arum and Roksa (2011) point out, "the average student studies less than two hours per day," but "55 percent have attained a B-plus grade point average or higher" (p. 88). If we accept that studying diligently is part of being a responsible student, we must also acknowledge that many students are not being held to account when they fail to live up to that responsibility.

What Should We Be Measuring?

How might we apply this principle of accountability to the components of social and personal responsibility discussed previously? We can learn from surveys whether our students espouse particular life goals, like becoming a community leader or an authority in one's field. To a lesser extent, we can document whether they engage in certain behaviors. But many colleges and universities make some kind of claim about producing responsible citizens.

If responsibility is a significant goal of higher education and if it implies being held accountable for the results of one's actions, then we should be assessing our level of success, both with current students and with alumni. This must include the documentation of behavior, not just values, and possibly even the effectiveness of that behavior.

We also need to promote a better balance of social responsibility with personal and academic responsibility. The five dimensions of the Core Commitments Initiative already include personal and academic responsibility. Without diminishing the importance of civic engagement, the higher education community should encourage a greater focus on such behaviors as striving for academic excellence by being a responsible student, on the kind of responsibility shown by raising a family and holding a job while going to college, and on the contributions to one's community made by running a business or holding an administrative job.

The life goals included in the personal responsibility factor are easy to operationalize. There are ways of identifying whether people have successfully raised families, run their own businesses, held administrative jobs, or become authorities in their fields. A few of the items in the social responsibility factor have the same quality: becoming a community leader, participating in community action, being involved in programs to clean up the environment. But what about "influencing social values"? It is unclear how we would know whether a student or a graduate had succeeded or failed at this pursuit, and it seems unlikely that failing to achieve such a goal would have repercussions for anyone at all. If responsibility is about being held accountable, failure in the personal responsibility sphere has far more obvious consequences than does failure in the social responsibility domain.

References

Arum, R., & Roksa, R. (2011). *Academically adrift: Limited learning on college campuses.* Chicago, IL: University of Chicago Press.

Trosset, C. (1998). Obstacles to open discussion and critical thinking. *Change, 30*(5), 44–49.

Carol Trosset is director of enrollment research at Bennington College in Bennington, VT.

New Directions for Higher Education • DOI:10.1002/he

4

*Understanding institutional climate enhances decision-
making capacity when planning new programs and improving
learning environments on college campuses. This chapter
defines climate, discusses the purpose and advantages of
climate assessment, and identifies important factors to
consider in planning and conducting a personal and social
responsibility climate assessment, using the Personal and
Social Responsibility Inventory as an example.*

Measuring Campus Climate for Personal and Social Responsibility

Andrew J. Ryder, Joshua J. Mitchell

Assisting in the development of students' personal and social responsibility
(PSR) is often considered an important aspect of higher learning. According
to the Association of American Colleges and Universities (AAC&U), an
organizational advocate for PSR and civic education, "ethical, civic, and
moral development should be closely tied to a substantive vision for student learning that is shared across constituent groups" (AAC&U, n.d., bul-
let point 4). Recently, the National Task Force on Civic Learning and
Democratic Engagement (2012) in its report, *A Crucible Moment: College
Learning and Democracy's Future*, reinforced the significance of this link to
student learning when it called for renewal of higher education's commitment to its civic and democratic mission. The National Task Force argued
that institutional leaders should renew this commitment by creating civic
investment plans that provide students opportunities for civic learning and
democratic engagement during their postsecondary education.

PSR is not a single outcome. It is not five outcomes, as might be
inferred from the five dimensions assessed by the Personal and Social
Responsibility Inventory (PSRI): striving for excellence, cultivating academic
integrity, contributing to a larger community, taking seriously the perspective of others, and developing competence in ethical and moral reasoning
and action. Instead, PSR is a set of related outcomes that are informed by
those five dimensions along with other areas related to civic learning, active
citizenship, and democratic engagement. Supporting the idea of PSR as a set of
outcomes of higher education, Ardaiolo, Neilson, and Daugherty (2011) and
O'Neill (2012) provided an overview of promising practices when
educating students for PSR. Ardaiolo and colleagues (2011) outlined how
two institutions worked to embed PSR into student life programs and
learning experiences on their respective campuses and identified promising

practices; O'Neill (2012) drew from multiple data sources to articulate the current status of PSR-related outcomes in higher education and provided an extensive look at promising practices.

Reason (2011) examined taking seriously the perspectives of others—an outcome of PSR—arguing that it should be an outcome of higher education because it "is essential to active citizenship in today's diverse democracy" (p. 1). He noted Dey and Associates' (2010) findings indicating that nearly 80% of campus professionals and 60% of students surveyed reported that they strongly agreed that taking seriously the perspectives of others should be a focus on their campus.

After establishing PSR as a set of outcomes, the emphasis necessarily shifts to determining how best to measure them. The approach taken by authors in this volume, and the institutions working with the PSRI, is to assess the developmental climate for PSR on a campus.

Climate is assumed to be a multifaceted concept that is not directly observable and difficult to measure (Hurtado, Griffin, Arellano, & Cuellar, 2008; Peterson & Spencer, 1990; Rankin & Reason, 2008; Tierney, 1990). In an attempt to measure climate, campus professionals and researchers often create constructs comprised of multiple attributes to assess climate—people's attitudes about, perceptions of, and experiences within a specified environment (Glisson & James, 2002; Hart & Fellabaum, 2008; Peterson & Spencer, 1990; Rankin & Reason, 2008). An institutional climate assessment can assist in determining whether—and how well—institutions provide educational environments that foster outcomes such as PSR and promote students' abilities to understand and act in accordance with these responsibilities. Climate assessment should serve as "a foundation for institutional change" (Hart & Fellabaum, 2008, p. 222). Also, climate assessment can provide a starting point for discussions about how to move toward creating, maintaining, or improving opportunities that promote student development and learning. It is important to note that for the purposes of this chapter we differentiate between climate, culture, and environment, even though many use these terms interchangeably in the literature (Glisson & James, 2002; Hart & Fellabaum, 2008; Peterson & Spencer, 1990).

A Brief History of Climate Assessment

During the latter part of the 20th century, climate assessment became a common concern among colleges and universities (Hart & Fellabaum, 2008; Shenkle, Snyder, & Bauer, 1998; Tierney, 1990). The use of campus climate assessments shifted from being reactive in nature to being a proactive assessment practice in an attempt to understand and address significant issues on campus and postsecondary education, more broadly (Hurtado et al., 2008). Moreover, research examining the results of climate assessment linked "the campus climate with key educational outcomes"

NEW DIRECTIONS FOR HIGHER EDUCATION • DOI:10.1002/he

(Hurtado et al., 2008, p. 204). The use of these assessments and the corresponding results increased in importance as the pressures mounted for both academic affairs and student affairs to engage in assessment and evidence-based practices and as administrators aimed to "identify areas for improvement to achieve educational goals" (Hurtado et al., 2008, p. 204).

Researchers in organizational behavior created an extensive literature base on organizational climate as it soared in popularity in the 1960s and 1970s. Peterson and Spencer (1990) stated that, although organizational literature provided a foundation for studying climate, research examining climate assessment in higher education was not as extensive as in organizational behavior. This could be because research on organizational climate has been conducted longer than research on the climate in postsecondary institutions (Peterson & Spencer, 1990). Another potential factor could be that researchers struggled with the definition and measurement of climate in the 1980s as pressures mounted to increase institutional effectiveness (Tierney, 1990).

Although strides have been made in the last few decades, assessing institutional climate remains a complex task requiring thoughtful design, measurement, and attention to the multiple factors affecting it (Hart & Fellabaum, 2008; Peterson & Spencer, 1990; Stodden, Brown, & Roberts, 2011; Tierney, 1990). In addition to accurate data collection and interpretation, researchers and campus professionals must have the ability to comprehend "a plethora of complex issues" (Stodden et al., 2011, p. 86). Moreover, Tierney (1990) stated climate is often difficult to understand because it seems "to defy precise definition and measurement" (p. 1). However, he urged his audience to remember that just "because variables are difficult to determine does not mean that we should ignore them" (p. 1).

Defining Climate

Although the terms environment, culture, and climate are used interchangeably by many (Glisson & James, 2002; Hart & Fellabaum, 2008; Peterson & Spencer, 1990), we differentiate them. In doing so, we acknowledge that although the terms are interconnected and provide a more complete understanding of the institution and its members, they are not the same. There seems to be a lack of consensus on a definition of climate (Glisson & James, 2002; Hart & Fellabaum, 2008; Peterson & Spencer, 1990). However, there is general agreement that climate is multifaceted, comprising items related to perceptions, attitudes, experiences, behaviors, expectations, standards, and levels of satisfaction. Although not all of these attributes are included in every climate study, researchers use these multiple sources to identify patterns based on responses from the current community members (Glisson & James, 2002; Hurtado et al., 2008; Peterson & Spencer, 1990; Rankin & Reason, 2008).

We define climate as a measure of people's attitudes about, perceptions of, and experiences within a specified environment (Glisson & James, 2002; Hart & Fellabaum, 2008; Peterson & Spencer, 1990; Rankin & Reason, 2008) and do not view it as the same thing as culture. Climate is measured through perceptions (Glisson & James, 2002; Peterson & Spencer, 1990; Rankin & Reason, 2008); culture is "the way things are done" (Glisson & James, 2002, p. 769)—the embedded patterns of behavior, shared values, assumptions, beliefs, or ideologies (Peterson & Spencer, 1990) as well as expectations (Glisson & James, 2002; Hurtado et al., 2008). Therefore, climate is in part a result of culture. "Thus, climate, compared to culture, is more concerned with current perceptions and attitudes rather than deeply held meanings, beliefs, and values" (Peterson & Spencer, 1990, p. 7).

Our discussion of climate refers to the campus environment for undergraduate students. More important, experiences within the campus environment are included as an element of climate because experiences affect many of the attributes of climate. Cress and Sax (1998) stated:

> We know that student values and attitudes are affected by the college experience. … Many of these changes in values and attitudes are not merely through normal maturation but are a result of attending college. This is indeed a welcome finding and one consistent with the original purposes of postsecondary liberal education. (p. 70)

We acknowledge that decision makers "need information about the complexities of their institutions' climates, that is, the interplay among people, processes, and institutional culture" to inform decision making, policies, and action (Baird, 1990, p. 35). After all, campus climate assessment should lead to and inform institutional change (Hart & Fellabaum, 2008).

Climate Assessment

Climate assessment is "the systematic measuring of effectiveness in an institution or program area so that an action plan for program improvement can be created and set in motion as a means of inducing change" (Nisonger Center, 2006a, 2006b, as cited in Stodden et al., 2011, p. 83). Climate data can be obtained through multiple methods depending on what questions are being asked. These methods encompass the traditional forms of qualitative and quantitative data collection (Hart & Fellabaum, 2008; Shenkle et al., 1998), including focus groups, face-to-face interviews, and web-based surveys depending on the nature of the question and the analytic approach.

Researchers and campus professionals assess climate to gain a better understanding of the prevailing attitudes and perceptions on campuses (Glisson & James, 2002; Hart & Fellabaum, 2008; Peterson & Spencer, 1990; Rankin & Reason, 2008) and promote institutional change (Hart &

Fellabaum, 2008). Campus assessments also provide a means of identifying gaps between constituents (Baird, 1990). Once those gaps are identified, steps can be taken to create new policies, procedures, and learning environments that support institutional aspirations. Before moving forward, it is important to understand where the institution is and where stakeholders want it to be.

Using Climate Assessment Data. Climate assessment data can deepen institutional knowledge and inform action by assisting researchers and campus professionals as they measure attitudes and behaviors and explore differences in perceptions among campus community members.

Measuring Attitudes and Behaviors. Measures of campus members' current attitudes, perceptions, behaviors, and expectations are essential to understanding and constructing climate (Baird, 1990; Glisson & James, 2002) as well as using that information to inform changes (Stodden et al., 2011). As defined earlier, climate is a measure of people's attitudes about, perceptions of, and experiences within a specified environment (Glisson & James, 2002; Hart & Fellabaum, 2008; Peterson & Spencer, 1990; Rankin & Reason, 2008). By measuring these items, campus professionals and researchers are better able to understand climate, which is typically seen as "an immeasurable construct" (Rankin & Reason, 2008, p. 264). These items—often found in surveys in the form of Likert-type scales (e.g., strongly disagree [1] to strongly agree [5])—measure perceptions of attitudes; however, some items ask respondents about their observable behaviors (Rankin & Reason, 2008). Once measured, campus professionals and researchers can use the data to gain a more complete understanding of the institutional climate and identify areas where action may be needed or beneficial.

Exploring Differences in Perceptions. In addition to providing a more in-depth understanding of the attitudes, perceptions, and behaviors of members of a campus community, campus climate data can be used "to compare [an] institution with similar colleges and universities in order to identify areas where changes are needed, make suggestions about how to improve the climate, and measure the effectiveness of these changes" (Baird, 1990, p. 35). For example, when institutional participants receive reports back after participating in surveys such as the Global Perspective Inventory, the National Survey of Student Engagement (NSSE), and the PSRI, the reports include information about how the institution compares to a selected set of institutions or a comparison between institutional scores and national scores.

In addition, data can be used to understand gaps between respondents' perceptions of campus climate and actual practices, as well as differences between subgroups of survey respondents (Baird, 1990). In these ways, assessment data can provide a meaningful starting point for dialogues aimed at change and can assist in identifying areas where partnerships may be formed in support of institutional goals. Winthrop University's vice president for student life Frank Ardaiolo used data from the PSRI to foster intentional partnerships between student affairs and academic affairs and build a culture of PSR on campus (Ardaiolo et al., 2011). In addition, Dey and Associates (2008) found that perceptions varied among and between the groups surveyed—campus professionals (i.e., academic administrators, faculty, and student affairs staff) and students depending on their status (i.e., first year, sophomore, junior, and senior).

Advantages of Climate Assessment. The many uses of climate assessment data also provide benefits to campus professionals. The assessment data can be used to inform decision making and to identify areas where action can have the greatest effect.

Inform Decision Making. When used appropriately, climate measures "offer great potential to enrich institutional statistics and action" (Stodden et al., 2011, p. 85). They also provide a means of informing the creation of policies and procedures (Baird, 1990), building relationships and meaningful partnerships between areas on campus (Ardaiolo et al., 2011), understanding the current attitudes and behaviors of community members (Rankin & Reason, 2008), and identifying areas of agreement and disagreement between and among groups (Baird, 1990). O'Neill (2012) provided an extensive look at how institutions can use the findings from climate surveys to inform practice. Among the seven recommendations she outlined, she encouraged campus professionals to be aware of opportunities on campus to inform decisions about what needs to be developed or maintained based on findings and institutional priorities. She also recommended identifying not only who does and does not choose to participate but also why. A key to understanding how an institution is progressing toward its goals, she said, is to assess along the way.

Identify Areas Where Action Can Have the Greatest Effect. "To stimulate action, a university might use [climate assessment] evidence to ameliorate the quality of instruction, perhaps by refining existing instructional methods and curricula" (Stodden et al., 2011, p. 85). Ardaiolo et al. (2011) provided examples of how two institutions used data from the PSRI to identify areas where they could best foster the development of PSR outcomes for students within and outside of the classroom. At Winthrop University, it was important for PSR to become part of the institutional experience, not merely a "token" project (Ardaiolo et al., 2011, p. 4). To have the greatest effect, PSR had to be engrained into the framework of the institution; it had to have buy-in at all levels. Winthrop students now encounter PSR in everything from their freshman seminar course to their capstone course as well as a customized common reader designed to introduce PSR. At Rollins College, peer educators (e.g., resident assistants, Greek life leaders, academic tutors, and peer mentors) were determined to be the best alternative to create a climate promoting PSR. Each educator received training related to PSR and was evaluated using a specifically designed matrix. Ardaiolo et al. (2011) reported Greek leaders at Rollins incorporated PSR into

Interfraternity Council and Pan-Hellenic Council, and peer mentors involved with first-year programs were required to complete three programs related to PSR.

Planning and Conducting a Climate Assessment for Personal and Social Responsibility

Considerations for planning and conducting a campus climate assessment are very similar to assessments for student learning or program effectiveness. The single best approach will be highly dependent on assessment goals and institutional needs, but it is clear that the assessments that yield the most actionable results involve planning prior to conducting the actual assessment. This section discusses key elements of planning and conducting a climate assessment. Exhaustive sources for planning and conducting assessments can be found in *Assessment Methods for Student Affairs* by John H. Schuh and Associates (2009) and *Program Evaluation: Alternative Approaches and Practical Guidelines* by Jody L. Fitzpatrick, James R. Sanders and Blaine R. Worthen (2011).

Planning for the Assessment. Assessment requires careful planning prior to data collection. The planning phase includes clarifying goals of the assessment, articulating assessment questions, identifying members of the campus community appropriately situated to serve as assessment participants, and finally choosing between developing a homegrown assessment or purchasing a published assessment tool (Cooper, 2009; Groves et al., 2009; Saunders & Cooper, 2009).

Clarifying Climate Assessment Goals. Any sort of assessment activity should be based on clearly defined goals. Is the goal to understand climate for PSR as perceived by a specifically defined group of students, such as on-campus residents or fraternity and sorority members? Or is the goal to gather a more holistic view for how faculty, staff, and students contribute to the overall climate for PSR? Similar to the assessment of learning outcomes, personnel charged with making changes based on climate assessment data, along with other key institutional constituents, should be involved in the process of determining climate assessment goals (Allen, 2006; Banta, 2004; Walvoord, 2004). Involving faculty and academic administrators, student affairs administrators, and institutional researchers may reveal specific campus needs or concerns to inform the goals of climate assessment. Clear goals simplify the process of developing specific questions to be answered by the assessment and the eventual selection of a climate assessment instrument (Saunders & Cooper, 2009).

Articulating Assessment Questions. Subsequent to the development of climate assessment goals is determining the questions to be answered through the assessment process. The nature of assessment questions determines whether a qualitative or quantitative assessment is most suitable and whether data collected will provide reflections on aspects of campus climate for PSR for a specified group or be more generalizable to the broader campus community. Both qualitative and quantitative data may provide deeper understandings of campus climate useful for improving climate for PSR. It is also important to consider the assessment questions and kind of data that will be most useful to institutional decision makers (Cooper, 2009; Saunders & Cooper, 2009).

Some assessment questions will be best answered through qualitative methods. For example, questions about individuals' conceptions of PSR or how organizational contexts have contributed to the climate for PSR would be best answered through interviews or focus groups with questions that elicit individual interpretations (Creswell, 2009; Jones, Torres, & Arminio, 2006). These methods are more likely than scale questions on a survey to yield rich, thick descriptions of specific ways that the campus climate supports aspects of PSR (Jones et al., 2006; Merriam, 1988). Although qualitative methods can collect highly detailed, contextualized data, it is usually difficult to collect data from large numbers of respondents and the analysis and interpretation of these data (e.g., transcribing and coding interview or focus group recordings) require substantial amounts of personnel time or money to pay for professional transcription services. Qualitative assessments are not concerned with generalizability beyond the group studied, but the trade-off is found in the power of their descriptive detail and explanations of particular phenomena (Creswell, 2009).

Survey instruments are frequently used to collect a range of quantitative data on college students (Cooper, 2009; Porter & Whitcomb, 2005; Saunders & Cooper, 2009; Umbach, 2004). Surveys such as the Cooperative Institutional Research Program and the NSSE are commonly used tools for gathering self-reported characteristics, beliefs, and indications of participation in curricular and cocurricular activities from college students. Some questions assessing climate for PSR are most appropriate for surveys. For example, data concerning which social or educational opportunities, campus services, members of the campus community, and the aspects of campus culture best support a climate for PSR could be collected using an inventory from which respondents choose those options that best apply to their experiences. Data about the degree to which different members of the campus community (e.g., students, faculty, or student affairs staff) promote a climate for PSR through certain practices may be collected by having respondents indicate their level of agreement with a series of statements about the behaviors of fellow community members. Although quantitative data lack the rich detail qualitative methods can provide, survey data can provide a breadth of information collected from large numbers of respondents, especially with the proliferation of web-based survey platforms (Umbach, 2004). Surveys using a probability sampling design representative of all members of the campus community can also yield results generalizable across the campus population (Groves et al., 2009).

Identifying Assessment Participants. It is important to collect assessment data from all the appropriate and relevant individuals; otherwise, the assessment is incomplete (Cooper, 2009). Suppose that fictional Urban Metro University (UMU), with undergraduate students living both on and off campus, launches a survey of students' perceptions of climate for PSR, but the assessment team collects data only from residence hall students. Students living in apartments off campus are excluded from the assessment, resulting in only a partial understanding of students' perceptions of the climate for PSR. In survey research, the group for whom a survey (or assessment) is intended is referred to as the target population (Groves et al., 2009). The target population can be further refined to explicitly describe the desired participants for the assessment, for example, all full-time undergraduate students who have been previously enrolled for at least one full term or all undergraduate faculty members, academic administrators, and student affairs staff. Whether the assessment is to be quantitative, like the UMU example, or qualitative, establishing parameters for assessment participants is a key consideration.

Choosing Between a Homegrown or Published Assessment Tool. A final step in planning a climate assessment for PSR is choosing the assessment tool. There are advantages and disadvantages in using a published tool or creating a new instrument. A homegrown assessment can be tailored to meet institutional needs and "allow for a more nuanced understanding of institution-specific programs" (Saunders & Cooper, 2009, p. 112). Conversely, a published assessment tool is more likely to allow for comparisons with national data and benchmarking across similar types of institutions. Either type of assessment can be used repeatedly over multiple assessment cycles to see how climate changes over time, as long as the instruments and questions remain unchanged (Cooper, 2009).

In addition to comparisons and benchmarking with other institutions, published instruments typically have significant advantages over homegrown assessment tools. Creating an assessment from scratch has inherent costs in terms of time and personnel costs that may exceed the price of purchasing a published instrument (Cooper, 2009). Whether using a quantitative or qualitative tool, developing a homegrown assessment requires that the instrument be pilot tested for clarity of directions, respondents' understanding of the questions, the length of time likely required to complete the assessment, and the presence of biased or offensive language (Colton & Covert, 2007; Cooper, 2009).

Quality, as indicated by validity and reliability, is a significant concern for homegrown survey instruments. Validity is an indication of how well an instrument measures what it purports to measure; reliability is an indication of how well the instrument assesses the same constructs time after time (Carmines & Zeller, 1979). Published assessment tools have usually been rigorously tested for validity and reliability and will include documentation of instrument quality. Publishers work with researchers who have expertise in both the design and the specific subject areas of the assessment to guarantee the integrity of their publications (Saunders & Cooper, 2009). Organizations marketing their own assessment tools should make available technical guides to their instruments for transparency and credibility.

A Final Step: Obtaining Approval for Research Involving Human Subjects. After the target population for the assessment has been identified and an assessment tool has been chosen, it is important to obtain approval from the campus office or committee that monitors human subjects research. Although it is unlikely that an assessment of campus climate for PSR will cause individuals harm, it is necessary to make certain the assessment is conducted within federal and institutional guidelines for studying human behavior. Human subjects approval protects the individuals being studied, those persons conducting the assessment, and the interests of the institution.

Conducting a Climate Assessment. Once the planning phase is completed, assessing campus climate for PSR begins with data collection, including setting a schedule for focus groups or interviews or survey administration. Once data are collected, data analysis and reporting of findings and recommendations conclude the process. Each of these activities benefits from care in the planning phase. Whether the assessment is qualitative or quantitative in nature, attention to detail is important to assessment success. This section briefly highlights some basic considerations for data collection, analysis, and reporting.

Data Collection. The target population identified for the assessment must be invited to participate in the assessment process. Typically personnel conducting qualitative assessments of campus climate might invite individuals who fit the definition of the target population to participate in focus groups or interviews. Such a general invitation may not yield adequate respondents, so it may be preferable to invite known individuals, such as student employees or students in leadership positions, who fit the target population definition to participate in an interview or focus group— otherwise known as convenience sampling (Gansemer-Topf & Wohlgemuth, 2009).

The most informative interviews and focus groups have some key features that yield good data. To create a space for open conversation and dialogue, the person conducting the interview or focus group must appear to be without judgment, be curious, and be able to connect participant comments back to the assessment questions. One or two focus group participants will often have more to say than others, so it is important that the interviewer work to respectfully encourage the involvement of other participants who may be more reserved. Interview or focus group questions that elicit a yes or no response usually fail to provide useful data and should be avoided. Questions that are too long or use jargon or advanced vocabulary may be more difficult for respondents to follow and answer correctly (Fitzpatrick et al., 2011).

New Directions for Higher Education • DOI:10.1002/he

Collecting quantitative assessment data using a survey also requires convincing members of the respective population to participate. Surveys usually include four to five contacts with planned participants, so the survey schedule should be set so as to avoid potentially conflicting or distracting events that may suppress response rates. The first contact for a survey assessment is a prenotification message sent by a recognizable person of authority announcing that the survey is coming and why it is important that individuals participate (Groves et al., 2009). Shortly after the prenotification, the survey is delivered. If the assessment uses a web-based survey, the survey is sent as a web link as part of the text of an email message. The final two or three contacts with potential participants occur as reminders to complete the survey (Cooper, 2009). Some assessment surveys may try to boost response rates through the use of incentives, such as a drawing for a new technological gadget or campus parking space, but it is unclear if these kinds of incentives significantly boost participation (Groves et al., 2009; Porter & Whitcomb, 2003).

Data Analysis. Qualitative and quantitative data analysis proceed very differently from one another, but both require substantial organizational efforts and diligent recording of decisions made in the analytic process about how different data will be used. Creswell (2009) outlined five broad steps for the analysis of qualitative data. First, organize and prepare interview or focus group data through sorting information by topic and creating a log to describe how data were collected (e.g., Who conducted the focus group and when and where did it occur? Who transcribed the recording?). Second, read through all the data collected to become familiar with or immersed in the data (Cooper & Shelley, 2009). Third, develop a coding process by initially identifying broader themes within the data and then breaking the themes into more specific ideas (Esterberg, 2002). The next step is to describe the participants and setting of the assessment to add context to the data. The fifth step is to interpret data by deciding what the data show and what has been learned through the assessment process.

A key organizational consideration for quantitative survey data is to make sure data are readable by computer. Web-based surveys usually provide data in a format readable by Microsoft Excel, SPSS, or other statistical software. Once the data are downloaded, a codebook should be created that matches survey items with the downloaded data points. The codebook should be used to track any changes in values assigned to data, decisions made to aggregate or combine data, and so forth (Cooper & Shelley, 2009). Simple descriptive statistics, such as item means (the average of all responses for an item) and item modes (the most common response to an item) and frequencies (number and percentage of respondents giving certain answers to an item) are helpful in gaining a basic understanding of survey results and may describe participants' perceptions of specific aspects of campus climate (Cooper & Shelley, 2009; Urdan, 2005). Additional analysis depends on the data available and the nature of the assessment questions. Tests for significant differences can be run to see if two distinct groups of students differ in their perceptions of certain items, such as those living on campus compared to those living off campus. Correlations and regressions can demonstrate relationships between items and multivariate regressions, and techniques like structural equation modeling can be employed to investigate predictive or causal relationship among different data points (Cooper & Shelley, 2009).

Results and Findings. The audience for the report of results and findings will determine the level of detail, depth of analysis and information provided, and the overall length of the report. Senior-level decision makers, given their range of responsibilities and time constraints, may read only an executive summary that highlights the most significant findings and recommendations. The assessment committee and units or departments participating in the assessment will likely want to read the full report (Fitzpatrick et al., 2011; Schuh, 2009). The best strategy to determine what to include in a report for a particular set of stakeholders is to ask them (Schuh, 2009).

Fitzpatrick et al. (2011) provide an outline for components of an assessment or evaluation report, including an executive summary; introduction and overview of the report that summarizes the purpose and limitations of the assessment; and details about the goals of the assessment, assessment questions, and the assessment plan. The outline also calls for a presentation of results that includes both a summary of findings and interpretation of findings. Recommendations for further study and for action steps based on the assessment should be featured prominently (Schuh, 2009). Action steps should be clearly linked to data to facilitate assessment-based improvements, otherwise known as "closing the loop" (Suskie, 2009, p. 65). Other considerations in writing the assessment report include avoiding jargon or technical language that may not be understood by the audience of the report, taking care not to single out individuals or areas if data reveal performance deficiencies, and using examples or illustrations to enhance the readability of the report.

The Personal and Social Responsibility Inventory: An Institutional Climate Measure

The PSRI provides an example of a quantitative survey designed to assess campus climate for PSR. The PSRI was developed under the auspices of the AAC&U as part of an initiative called "Core Commitments: Educating Students for Personal and Social Responsibility," asserting PSR as critical outcomes of college (AAC&U, n.d.; PSRI, n.d.). The initial inventory was developed in 2006. This section provides a brief overview of the PSRI as a tool for assessing campus climate for PSR, highlighting the goals and purpose of the PSRI, development of the PSRI, forms and format of the inventory, the data collection process, and analytic reports provided by the PSRI.

New Directions for Higher Education • DOI:10.1002/he

Purpose of the PSRI. The PSRI was designed to measure campus climate along five dimensions of PSR. These dimensions were developed through rigorous research in student development theory and organizational and campus climates conducted in 2006 by cognitive psychologist L. Lee Knefelkamp of Teacher's College, Columbia University, in consultation with Richard Hersh of the Council for Aid to Education and with the research assistance of Lauren Ruff. The dimensions of the PSRI have since been refined first by Eric L. Dey of the University of Michigan Center for the Study of Higher and Postsecondary Education and later by Robert D. Reason of Iowa State University's Research Institute for Studies in Education (RISE; PSRI, n.d.). The five dimensions assessed by the PSRI are:

Striving for excellence. Striving for excellence is defined as having a strong work ethic and a commitment to doing one's best in every aspect of college.

Cultivating academic integrity. Institutions that cultivate academic integrity encourage members of the community to act out of honesty, fairness, and respect for others and may include participating in a formally established academic honor code.

Contributing to a larger community. Contributing to a larger community means acknowledging and acting on a sense of responsibility to the local, national, and global community.

Taking seriously the perspective of others. Institutional climates that encourage perspective taking help community members learn how to make informed judgments, including engaging with diverse perspectives and points of view.

Developing competence in ethical and moral reasoning and action. In this dimension, institutional climates help community members incorporate the other four dimensions as part of ethical decision making as part of all learning and living experiences.

Each of these five dimensions is based on one or more groups of survey items or factors.

Development of the PSRI. The PSRI was developed drawing on literature in student development, survey research, and psychological measurement. Measures of personal qualities related to PSR were linked to frequently studied elements of campus and organizational climate thought to support these qualities. These elements of climate include mission and educational purpose of the institution, institutional leadership and policies, campus activities and organizations, academic opportunities, curricula, teaching, and reward systems (Barnhart, Antonaros, Holsapple, Ott, & Dey, 2010). The five dimensions as well as individual survey items that form their underlying factors were produced through this review of literature.

The PSRI has been repeatedly tested to verify that individual items and the survey as a whole measure campus climate for PSR. The PSRI was pilot tested for readability and usability. Reliability testing has confirmed the stability of the factors that make up the five dimensions as well as individual survey items. Validity testing via expert consultation has demonstrated that the PSRI measures PSR (content validity). Validity testing using factor analysis has tested the relationships between the dimensions and individual survey items and shown consistency in the strength and direction of these relationships (Barnhart et al., 2010). Such rigorous testing demonstrates instrument quality and credibility (Groves et al., 2009).

PSRI Forms and Format.   There are two versions of the PSRI: one for students and one for campus professionals. The student survey is intended for any undergraduate student aged 18 or older, enrolled either full time or part time, living on or off campus. The campus professionals form of the survey is intended for student affairs professionals (not student staff members), academic administrators (from the president or chancellor through administrative staff within academic departments), and faculty members (any faculty member with undergraduate teaching responsibilities, including adjuncts; Barnhart et al., 2010). These definitions of student and campus professionals make up the population frame for the PSRI (Groves et al., 2009). By soliciting participation from these two broadly defined groups, the PSRI is designed to provide a holistic picture of campus climate for PSR.

Both forms of the survey include a series of demographic questions, such as race, gender, sex, and academic major or department. The survey is then divided into five sections, one for each dimension of PSR. Each of these sections includes a group of items using an agreement scale (Disagree Strongly to Strongly Agree) asking respondents to assess how others within the institution (e.g., students, faculty, student affairs professionals) support that specific dimension of PSR, whether that dimension is a focus of the institution and whether it ought to be a focus of the institution. Using the same agreement scale, respondents are also asked about their own behaviors relative to the dimension. Each section of the survey concludes with an open-ended question giving respondents a chance to write about one or more personal experiences on campus relative to the dimension (AAC&U, 2011a, 2011b).

Assessing Campus Climate Using the PSRI.   The PSRI is managed by a project team at RISE at Iowa State University who work with individual institutions that elect to use the PSRI as an assessment tool for campus climate. The PSRI team helps participating institutions determine who should be invited to participate in the PSRI as part of the climate assessment, given differences in student and campus professional determinations that may exist across different institutional types. The PSRI team also works with participating institutions to develop a schedule for survey administration. Because the PSRI is a web-based survey, the team also coordinates distribution of the survey and assists with any troubleshooting that may be required.

Survey Administration and Data Collection. The PSRI team works with the participating institution to develop a 21-day schedule for administering the PSRI. The PSRI is usually administered in the spring of the year, so institutional schedules are constructed to avoid spring break and major campus events during this time of year. The PSRI team also advises the participating institution on working with information technology personnel to make sure campus servers treat the survey as normal electronic mail and encourages participating institutions to advertise the survey on campus so students and campus professionals recognize the PSRI as a credible activity.

Consistent with established survey research methods, the PSRI is administered using five email contacts with participants (Cooper & Shelley, 2009). The first contact is a prenotification message, usually from the institution president, vice president for student affairs, or other recognizable leader. Within 36 hours after delivery of the prenotification, an email message is sent to all participants inviting them to participate in the survey and this message is followed by three reminder messages to nonresponders. The PSRI team apprises the participating institution of response rates as well as any problems experienced during survey administration.

Before data are analyzed, the research team compares student survey response rates by race, sex, and class year with the percentages of students invited to participate by race, sex, and class year. Weights, called nonresponse weights, are then calculated and applied so that survey data are representative of the institution (Groves et al., 2009). Research has demonstrated that race, sex, and class year may influence likelihood of survey response (Dey, 1997; Porter & Whitcomb, 2005). Weighting is a common postsurvey adjustment routine to compensate for survey nonresponse and improve survey estimates for groups underrepresented in survey data (Groves et al., 2009).

Analytic Reports and Data Sets. PSRI participating institutions receive an analytic report as well as raw survey data following completion of the survey. Quantitative data in the analytic reports include item frequencies (counts and percentages), item means and standard deviations for the institution and for the national set of PSRI participating institutions, and computed factor scores for the groups of items contributing to each dimension of PSR assessed by the PSRI. Institutional and national factor scores and student and campus professional factors scores are all presented side by side for purposes of comparison. Narrative data consist of text responses to open-ended questions in the survey, and these data may shed light on how institutional events or circumstances shape quantitative results.

The PSRI team also provides participating institutions with a raw data set of student responses to the PSRI, including calculated nonresponse weights. The student data set includes identifying information so that institutions can link PSRI data to other assessment and student record data for additional analysis. The campus professionals data set does not include identifying information; as an extra measure to preserve confidentiality, campus professionals data are aggregated when fewer than five individuals of an identifiable demographic category within a department or unit are represented in the data (e.g., four Latino chemistry faculty). Participating institutions report that the raw data from the PSRI campus climate assessment is most valuable to them.

Conclusion

If educating students for PSR is an important aspect of higher learning, determining whether campus climates support PSR education and measuring PSR-related outcomes must be included on institutional assessment agendas. Not only do assessment data improve our understanding of student learning and institutional outcomes, they provide the evidence to argue for changes and improvements to how we teach and engage with students (Hart & Fellabaum, 2008). Campus programs promoting civic learning, democratic engagement, global citizenship, community service, personal excellence, and academic integrity certainly contribute to the student experience and institutional climate for PSR; assessment data tell us how.

Because the concepts related to PSR can be challenging to operationalize and assess, planning for assessment is critical. Determining assessment goals, articulating assessment questions, identifying participants, and choosing between homegrown or published tools are all steps toward an effective strategy for PSR or other types of assessment. Although the PSRI provides a rigorously tested, web-based survey yielding quantitative and narrative data, the choice of assessments should be guided by institutional needs.

References

Allen, M. J. (2006). *Assessing general education programs.* San Francisco, CA: Anker.

Ardaiolo, F. P., Neilson, S., & Daugherty, T. K. (2011). Teaching students personal and social responsibility with measurable learning outcomes. *Journal of College and Character, 12*(2), 1–9. doi:10.2202/1940-1639.1781

Association of American Colleges and Universities (AAC&U). (2011a). *Personal and Social Responsibility Inventory, campus professionals edition.* Washington, DC: Author.

Association of American Colleges and Universities (AAC&U). (2011b). *Personal and Social Responsibility Inventory, student edition.* Washington, DC: Author.

Association of American Colleges and Universities (AAC&U). (n.d.). *Core commitments: Educating students for personal and social responsibility.* Retrieved from http://www.aacu.org/core_commitments/philosophy.cfm

Baird, L. L. (1990). Campus climate: Using surveys for policy-making. In W. G. Tierney (Ed.), *New Directions for Institutional Research: No. 68.* Assessing academic climates and cultures (pp. 35–46). San Francisco, CA: Jossey-Bass.

Banta, T. W. (2004). Introduction: What are some hallmarks of effective practice in assessment? In T. W. Banta (Ed.), *Hallmarks of effective outcomes assessment* (pp. 1–8). San Francisco, CA: Jossey-Bass.

Barnhart, C., Antonaros, M., Holsapple, M. A., Ott, M. C., & Dey, E. L. (2010). *The PSRI technical guide.* Washington, DC: Association of American Colleges and Universities.

Carmines, E. G., & Zeller, R. A. (1979). *Reliability and validity assessment.* Thousand Oaks, CA: Sage.

Colton, D., & Covert, R. W. (2007). *Designing and constructing instruments for social research and evaluation.* San Francisco, CA: Jossey-Bass.

Cooper, R. M. (2009). Planning for and implementing data collection. In J. H. Schuh (Ed.), *Assessment methods for student affairs* (pp. 51–75). San Francisco, CA: Jossey-Bass.

Cooper, R. M., & Shelley, M. C. (2009). Data analysis. In J. H. Schuh (Ed.), *Assessment methods for student affairs* (pp. 141–169). San Francisco, CA: Jossey-Bass.

Cress, C. M., & Sax, L. J. (1998). Campus climate issues to consider for the next decade. In K. W. Bauer (Ed.), *New Directions for Institutional Research: No. 98. Campus climate: Understanding the critical components of today's colleges and universities* (pp. 65–80). San Francisco, CA: Jossey-Bass.

Creswell, J. W. (2009). *Research design: Qualitative, quantitative, and mixed methods approaches* (3rd ed.). Los Angeles, CA: Sage.

Dey, E. L. (1997). Working with low survey response rates: The efficacy of weighting adjustments. *Research in Higher Education, 38*(2), 215–227.

Dey, E. L., & Associates. (2008). *Should colleges focus more on personal and social responsibility?* Washington, DC: Association of American Colleges and Universities.

Dey, E. L., & Associates. (2010). *Engaging diverse viewpoints: What is the campus climate for perspective-taking?* Washington, DC: Association of American Colleges and Universities.

Esterberg, K. G. (2002). *Qualitative methods in social science research.* Boston, MA: McGraw-Hill.

Fitzpatrick, J. L., Sanders, J. R., & Worthen, B. R. (2011). *Program evaluation: Alternative approaches and practical guidelines* (4th ed.). Boston, MA: Pearson.

Gansemer-Topf, A., & Wohlgemuth, D. R. (2009). Selecting, sampling, and soliciting subjects. In J. H. Schuh (Ed.), *Assessment methods for student affairs* (pp. 77–105). San Francisco, CA: Jossey-Bass.

Glisson, C., & James, L. R. (2002). The cross-level effects of culture and climate in human services teams. *Journal of Organizational Behavior, 23,* 767–794. doi:10.1002/job.162

Groves, R. M., Fowler, F. J., Couper, M. P., Lepkowski, J. M., Singer, E., & Tourangeau, R. (2009). *Survey Methodology* (2nd ed.). Hoboken, NJ: Wiley.

Hart, J., & Fellabaum, J. (2008). Analyzing campus climate studies: Seeking to define and understand. *Journal of Diversity in Higher Education, 1,* 222–234. doi:10.1037/a0013627

Hurtado, S., Griffin, K. A., Arellano, L., & Cuellar, M. (2008). Assessing the value of climate assessments: Progress and future directions. *Journal of Diversity in Higher Education, 1,* 204–221. doi:10.1037/a0014009

Jones, S. R., Torres, V., & Arminio, J. (2006). *Negotiating the complexities of qualitative research in higher education.* New York, NY: Routledge.

Merriam, S. B. (1988). *Case study research in education: A qualitative approach.* San Francisco, CA: Jossey-Bass.

National Task Force on Civic Learning and Democratic Engagement. (2012). *A crucible moment: College learning and democracy's future.* Retrieved from http://www.aacu.org/civic_learning/crucible/documents/crucible_508F.pdf

O'Neill, N. (2012). *Promising practices for personal and social responsibility: Findings from a national research collaborative.* Washington, DC: Association of American Colleges and Universities.

Personal and Social Responsibility Inventory (PSRI). (n.d.). *About the PSRI.* Association of American Colleges and Universities. Retrieved from http://www.psri.hs.iastate.edu/

Peterson, M. W., & Spencer, M. G. (1990). Understanding academic culture and climate. In W. G. Tierney (Ed.), *New Directions for Institutional Research: No. 68. Assessing academic climates and cultures* (pp. 3–34). San Francisco, CA: Jossey-Bass.

Porter, S. R., & Whitcomb, M. E. (2003). The impact of lottery incentives on student survey response rates. *Research in Higher Education, 44*(4), 309–407.

Porter, S. R., & Whitcomb, M. E. (2005). Non-response in student surveys: The role of demographics, engagement, and personality. *Research in Higher Education, 46*(2), 127–152.

Rankin, S., & Reason, R. (2008). Transformational tapestry model: A comprehensive approach to transforming campus climate. *Journal of Diversity in Higher Education, 1*(4), 262–274. doi:10.1037/a0014018

Reason, R. D. (2011). Expanding the conversation: Perspective taking as a civic outcome of college. *Journal of College and Character, 12*(2), 1–6. doi:10.2202/1940-1639.1786

Saunders, K., & Cooper, R. M. (2009). Instrumentation. In J. H. Schuh (Ed.), *Assessment methods for student affairs* (pp. 107–139). San Francisco, CA: Jossey-Bass.

Schuh, J. H. (2009). Writing reports and conducting briefings. In J. H. Schuh (Ed.), *Assessment methods for student affairs* (pp. 171–189). San Francisco, CA: Jossey-Bass.

Schuh, J. H., & Associates. (2009). *Assessment methods for student affairs.* San Francisco, CA: Jossey-Bass.

Shenkle, C. W., Snyder, R. S., & Bauer, K. W. (1998). Measures of campus climate. In K. W. Bauer (Ed.), *New Directions for Institutional Research: No. 98. Campus climate: Understanding the critical components of today's colleges and universities* (pp. 81–99). San Francisco, CA: Jossey-Bass.

Stodden, R. A., Brown, S. E., & Roberts, K. (2011). Disability-friendly university environments: Conducting a climate assessment. In W. S. Harbour & J. W. Madaus (Eds.), *New Directions for Higher Education: No. 154. Disability services and campus dynamics* (pp. 83–92). San Francisco, CA: Jossey-Bass. doi:10.1002/he.437

Suskie, L. (2009). *Assessing student learning: A common sense guide* (2nd ed.). San Francisco, CA: Jossey-Bass.

Tierney, W. G. (1990). Editor's note. In W. G. Tierney (Ed.), *New Directions for Institutional Research: No. 68. Assessing academic climates and cultures* (pp. 1–2). San Francisco, CA: Jossey-Bass.

Umbach, P. D. (2004). Web surveys: Best practices. In S. R. Porter (Ed.), *New Directions for Institutional Research: No. 121. Overcoming survey research problems* (pp. 23–38). San Francisco, CA: Jossey-Bass.

Urdan, T. C. (2005). *Statistics in plain English.* Mahwah, NJ: Lawrence Erlbaum Associates, Inc.

Walvoord, B. E. (2004). *Assessment clear and simple: A practical guide for institutions, departments, and general education.* San Francisco, CA: Jossey-Bass.

ANDREW J. RYDER is assistant professor of higher education at the University of North Carolina, Wilmington. He previously served as project director for the Personal and Social Responsibility Inventory at Iowa State University.

JOSHUA J. MITCHELL is a graduate research assistant at the Research Institute for Studies in Education (RISE) and a doctoral student at Iowa State University's School of Education with a concentration in higher education.

5

This chapter highlights good practices and lessons learned for infusing personal responsibility—striving for excellence, cultivating academic integrity, and developing competence in ethical and moral reasoning and action—as outcomes of college.

Infusing Personal Responsibility into the Curriculum and Cocurriculum: Campus Examples

Nancy O'Neill

This chapter highlights curricular and cocurricular practices related to personal responsibility, particularly the Core Commitments dimensions of cultivating personal and academic integrity and developing competence in ethical and moral reasoning. The practices come from campuses that took part in the Core Commitments leadership consortium from 2007 to 2009. The 23 institutions selected for the consortium came into Core Commitments with strengths in particular personal and social responsibility (PSR) dimensions based on their institutional histories and priorities. This enabled different consortium members to serve as "resident experts" on different dimensions. At the same time, all of the consortium members recognized the need to broaden and deepen their existing efforts to engage more students, over time, and across their educational experiences. This recognition was their impetus to join the consortium and formed the basis for the work they accomplished over the course of the initiative and beyond.

Context

The leadership consortium campuses spent part of their first year in the Core Commitments Initiative administering the Personal and Social Responsibility Inventory (PSRI), a campus climate survey that was developed to assess the perceptions of respondents regarding opportunities for education for PSR. If the consortium members had suspected coming in that there was a desire and a need to go broader and deeper with respect to

NEW DIRECTIONS FOR HIGHER EDUCATION, no. 164, Winter 2013 © Wiley Periodicals, Inc.
Published online in Wiley Online Library (wileyonlinelibrary.com) • DOI:10.1002/he.20075

their curricular and cocurricular offerings, the PSRI confirmed these beliefs.

The survey results indicated widespread desire for a focus on PSR outcomes on the part of both campus professionals and students. For example, nearly nine out of 10 campus professionals and seven out of 10 students who completed the survey strongly agreed that personal and academic integrity should be a major focus of their institution, whereas more than two-thirds of campus professionals and more than half of students strongly agreed that developing competence in ethical and moral reasoning should be a major institutional focus (Dey & Associates, 2010). This finding complements other recent findings suggesting that interest in personal responsibility is strong. Data from the 2007 Higher Education Research Institute Faculty Survey, for instance, indicate that 70% of 4-year faculty believe it is "essential" or "very important" to help students develop their moral character, an increase of 13 percentage points from 2004. Similarly, the data indicate that two-thirds of 4-year faculty believe it is "essential" or "very important" to help students develop their personal values, an increase of 15 percentage points from 2004 (DeAngelo, Hurtado, Pryor, Santos, & Korn, 2009). In terms of larger institutional vision, too, a recent survey of Association of American Colleges and Universities (AAC&U) member campuses indicate that 78% of responding institutions had ratified a set of learning goals for undergraduates, and within this group, 75% included ethical reasoning among these outcomes (Peter Hart & Associates, 2009).

These data signal a robust endorsement of personal responsibility as a goal of undergraduate education, but enacting this goal comprehensively across programs may be where the harder work lies. According to the 2007 PSRI findings, only four out of 10 students and a similar number of campus professionals strongly agreed that personal and academic integrity currently was a major focus of their institution. Even fewer students and campus professionals—one-quarter and one-third, respectively—strongly agreed that moral and ethical reasoning currently was a major institutional focus (Dey & Associates, 2010).

When the authors of the study looked more closely at curricular and cocurricular offerings, they found indications of success as well as work that remained in making personal responsibility pervasive across campuses. For example, nearly eight out of 10 students and almost as many campus professionals reported that course syllabi frequently define academic dishonesty, including such issues as plagiarism, improper citation of Internet sources, buying papers from others, and cheating on assignments or tests. Moreover, a strong majority of students and campus professionals strongly agreed that faculty understood, supported, and reinforced the academic honesty policies of the campus. However, far fewer—about one-third of students and one-fourth of campus professionals—strongly agreed that these same academic honesty policies actually help stop cheating. When it came to opportunities for students to further develop their capacities for ethical and moral reasoning, only roughly one-third of students and campus professionals reported that formal courses frequently provide opportunities for students to further develop these capacities, and only slightly higher percentages reported that out-of-class activities frequently provide opportunities for students to further develop these capacities. Only 21% of students strongly agreed that the importance of developing ethical and moral reasoning was frequently communicated to students by the institution (Dey & Associates, 2010).

It was important to emphasize to the leadership consortium schools that these findings represented the perceptions of various constituents across campus. The quantitative data did not indicate why constituents responded as they did. In year one of the consortium, the leadership campuses undertook analyses of their own data, including qualitative responses in the survey, and held campus dialogues to begin to answer the question "why?" for themselves. The institutions also began a process of mapping PSR-related activities using a matrix that was developed for the initiative, to better understand whether identified gaps were due to a lack of awareness about existing programs and practices related to PSR, a lack of impact of these programs and practices on the overall institutional culture, or actual gaps in programs and practices.

Using their proposed projects as a starting point and informed by their PSRI findings, institutions in the leadership consortium entered into an intensive period of activity and produced an array of tangible curricular and cocurricular innovations and interventions. These included new emphases in general education, advising, orientation, first-year programs, and leadership programs; PSR-specific assignments in high-enrollment courses; minigrant opportunities that required collaboration between faculty and student affairs professionals; the development of capstone courses; peer mentoring programs and faculty-to-faculty consulting; and the use of online as well as face-to-face platforms to continue campus conversations about PSR goals. The remainder of this chapter focuses on campus examples of these innovations and interventions and ends with a summary of several lessons learned across these specific campus contexts. The campuses examples are meant to suggest a range of replicable activities for other campuses looking to boost personal responsibility activities; the sample is not an exhaustive rendering of the work of the leadership consortium in these areas. The information included comes from the institutions' initial proposals and other supporting documents as well as from interviews with the team leaders conducted in June 2012.

California State University, Northridge: Academic Integrity and Financial Responsibility

One of the largest institutions in the Core Commitments leadership consortium, California State University, Northridge (CSUN) enrolled nearly

27,000 undergraduates in 2007. CSUN is also a federally designated Minority Serving Institution and Hispanic Serving Institution, and at the start of the Core Commitments project, more than 54% of CSUN students received financial aid (California State University Northridge, 2007).

CSUN's work in personal responsibility concentrated on academic and personal integrity, including a focus on financial responsibility and debt management. According to Adam Swenson, associate professor of philosophy and one of the CSUN team leaders, these choices were strategic. Among the five dimensions of PSR, personal and academic integrity was an area about which faculty and student affairs staff "already felt passionate," Swenson said, "but there was a deficit of knowledge about what it really involved." Furthermore, the project was launching just as the financial crisis was exploding in California in 2008. "There were anecdotal reports of students living in their cars, students were facing increases in tuition, and our Freshman Common Reading Program had selected the Barbara Ehrenreich book, *Nickel and Dimed*, for the freshman common reading," Swenson said. "People could see the need for [a focus on financial responsibility] and we thought that it would be relatively easy to create explicit assignments about this."

The main strategy the CSUN team used to launch a focus on personal and academic integrity was to build on what colleagues were already doing and to look at where they could have maximum impact in terms of reaching students. This led the team to focus on CSUN's freshman composition programs, which had already taken root across campus in departments such as Pan-African Studies and Chicana/o Studies. The goals of the freshman composition programs—developing students into critical readers and writers—would complement a focus on personal and academic integrity as a content area with which students could grapple. "The goal was to use those writing assignments to get students thinking about things their teachers already thought were important," Swenson said. "We approached the [freshman composition programs] teachers by simply asking, 'How about adding in a couple of assignments on these topics?'" Meanwhile, the dean of students, who was a member of CSUN's Core Commitments team, worked to connect these faculty with existing campus resources to support the group undertaking these new assignments. The CSUN team developed a set of writing prompts that freshman composition programs faculty could easily incorporate and adapt to their specific courses (see Appendix 5.1). This turned out to be another key to wider adoption. "We encouraged people to modify [the prompts] and to let us know what they did," Swenson said.

As can be seen in Appendix 5.1, the initial writing prompts concentrated on common dilemmas facing CSUN students as well as broader, complex topics that demanded substantial reflection. Prompts ranged from a few sentences to almost a page in length, often incorporating national statistics and current events on campus and in the larger society (see Appendix 5.2). These materials were soon augmented by prompts developed within particular programs. "Before long, we had the material in an original resource guide," said Swenson, "and then a set of resources that were germane to faculty members' specific course goals."

Overall, Swenson noted, the prompts were designed to help students realize that cultivating integrity is an active, self-conscious process. "We aimed to develop assignments that would help students see that many everyday decisions shouldn't just be made on the basis of how they happen to feel at the moment," Swenson said. "We wanted to help them develop a habit of consciously looking for the ethical issues present in a decision, thinking through the potential consequences, and acting in ways that are consistent with their sense of who they are and the sort of person they want to be."

According to Swenson, the prompts continue to be used in CSUN's Writing Reading Across Disciplines (WRAD) courses today. Though CSUN has experienced significant budget cuts since 2007 that have directly affected the WRAD program, Swenson said there are other lasting benefits that resulted from this work as well. WRAD program directors "got into the habit of developing things together," he said, "and it's easier to get people together now around a common goal."

University of Central Florida: "Z" Grade Designation, Integrity Seminars and Modules, and Faculty Development

The University of Central Florida (UCF) entered the Core Commitments project with an aim to make activities related to ethics and academic integrity more pervasive across a student body that in 2007 comprised nearly 40,000 undergraduates and 7,000 graduate students. The institution looked to engage both its research and its teaching functions in this work and to create programming for both students and faculty. The institution also looked to policy development as a way to reinforce ethics and academic integrity, including through its standing Ethics Task Force within the faculty senate. The task force is charged with developing and advising the university on institutional rules, policies, and procedures for academic community standards (University of Central Florida, 2007).

During the Core Commitments project, UCF leaders began looking at a policy intervention that could be used by faculty in cases where students were found in violation of academic integrity policies. The goal was to create a policy tool that prioritized educating students rather than simply punishing them. After significant dialogue involving faculty, students, and student affairs professionals, UCF developed and launched a "Z" grade designation in 2010. In cases where a student was found in violation of academic integrity policies, a faculty member had the option to attach a "Z" designation to the student's grade in the course. In the case of a first-time "Z" designation, students could satisfactorily complete a mandatory, noncredit academic integrity seminar and repeat the course. Upon doing so, and upon satisfactorily completing the course a second time, the "Z" designation would be removed. In the case of a second "Z" designation, students would also need to complete the mandatory academic integrity seminar, but the "Z" designation would become a permanent notation on the student's transcript.

In 2011, UCF reviewed the procedure and the educational program attached to the designation and made the designation mandatory for all academic misconduct cases reported by faculty. According to Patricia MacKown, associate vice president for student development and enrollment services, and Nancy Stanlick, assistant dean in the College of Arts and Humanities, this policy has had the intended impact. "Of all of the 'Zs' that have been put on students' grades since the policy began, only one has stayed on," MacKown said. Stanlick added, "Recidivism has declined not just because of the 'Z' itself but because of the education that comes with it."

During the Core Commitments project, the UCF team also focused on creating more proactive educational vehicles to complement the seminars attached to the "Z" designation. Specifically, the team spearheaded the creation of three proactive, required academic integrity modules, "Maintaining Academic Integrity," "Tips for Success in Academic Integrity," and "Consequences," which must be satisfactorily completed by students before they can register for their first semester of classes. According to MacKown, the modules take about 15 minutes to complete and contain short scenarios where an incoming student walks through issues he or she would typically encounter related to academic integrity. Students working on the modules then work through a set of questions that reflect a set of embedded learning outcomes. Students must score an 80% or above or they must redo the module. "We started with a discussion of what we wanted students to take away from this [kind of intervention]," MacKown said. "Then we wrote learning outcomes and scripted scenarios." MacKown said this initial work has spurred more specific requests for modules tailored to niche groups that may face particular challenges in relation to academic integrity, such as international students and graduate students. Indeed, more recently, the modules have been expanded to include transfer students, and they are now being retooled for graduate students to focus on research ethics. Incoming faculty also now view the modules and discuss the issues raised in them in relation to helping students develop a strong foundation in academic ethics and integrity.

The UCF Core Commitments project also sponsored an extended faculty development effort related to academic ethics. In 2007, the UCF team sponsored a track in both the summer and the winter faculty development conferences, which are held every year. Cohorts of faculty developed related content for courses ranging from philosophy and political science to health professions and engineering. In 2008, the team launched a course innovation project focused on faculty developing modules for other faculty. Titled "What Every Faculty Member and Every Student Should Know about Academic

Ethics," the modules were then showcased during UCF's summer 2008 faculty development conference (see Appendix 5.3).

UCF's work to make academic integrity a pervasive part of the campus culture has pointed out some additional areas in need of great attention and research. One such area is the way in which online teaching environments may change both students' perceptions of what constitutes inappropriate academic conduct and how faculty might rethink and restructure assignments to steer students away from simple information retrieval from electronic sources, for example. Overall, both Stanlick and MacKown stressed the need for a positive orientation in the work and for planning for constant change. "It's about how to approach a discipline with integrity, versus how to avoid dishonesty," Stanlick said. "It's never over," MacKown added. "We are continuously reviewing and tweaking and reviewing again. That's why assessment is so important—we need to know if and what students are learning rather than simply creating programs that make us feel good."

The University of Alabama at Birmingham: Ethics and Civic Responsibility (ECR) Course Designations and Capstones

When the University of Alabama at Birmingham (UAB) entered into the Core Commitments in 2007, the institution's proposed work was guided by a larger Quality Enhancement Plan (QEP) that had been developed in 2005 for its reaccreditation by the Southern Association of Colleges and Schools. Through the QEP, the institution would "[hold] itself accountable for introducing, reinforcing, practicing, and assessing three competencies targeted for initial enhancement: writing, quantitative literacy, and ethics and civic responsibility" (University of Alabama at Birmingham, 2007). ECR, in turn, was defined as a multifaceted construct that includes responsible moral reasoning in everyday life and in students' chosen disciplines, as well as sensitivity to and respect for diverse opinions of others, knowledgeable decision-making, and responsible engagement in the community" (University of Alabama at Birmingham, 2007). Although UAB had many curricular and cocurricular offerings related to ethics and civic responsibility for its more than 11,000 undergraduate students, there was an expressed interest in creating more intentional curricular pathways for all students related to the three QEP outcome areas. These pathways would begin from a newly created first-year program, include intensive ECR designated courses, and culminate with senior experiences in the majors. Today, UAB has both midlevel ECR-designated courses and capstones that include ethics and civic responsibility as a learning goal.

According to Marilyn Kurata, the Core Commitments team leader and then director of core curriculum enhancement in the Office of Undergraduate Programs, the key to the curricular change that occurred was to ensure that the process was squarely in the purview of faculty. "The source of why

NEW DIRECTIONS FOR HIGHER EDUCATION • DOI:10.1002/he

we were able to do this, and it took years…it had to be generated by faculty," said Kurata. The Core Commitments team, which also worked directly on the QEP efforts, began by approaching individual faculty and departments that already had ethical and moral reasoning embedded in disciplinary standards, such as philosophy, business, sociology, and nursing. Well-respected faculty members from these disciplines joined with Kurata and colleagues from student affairs to form an ECR committee, which started small and grew over time.

The group began by gathering, discussing, and vetting definitions of ethics and civic responsibility for the purpose of creating outcome statements. These discussions "were hugely valuable," Kurata said. "Members went back and discussed definitions with colleagues, and this began to familiarize faculty with the idea and terminology of ECR." When the group took these discussions out to the rest of campus, "people weren't taken by surprise." Another belief that the group nurtured through the QEP experience was that ECR "had to be both curricular and cocurricular," Kurata said. The QEP, she said, "broke down silos and promoted shared responsibility." This concept of campus partnerships was exemplified by the campus book program, which annually engaged faculty, staff, students, and administrators from around campus in dialogues on ethical and social issues.

The ECR committee, now comprising a significant number of departments across campus, concentrated on "how ethics and ethical reasoning were or should be a part of every disciplinary major," Kurata said. The key here was to acknowledge that what this might look like in one discipline could be very different from the focus in another discipline. "We asked every department and program to be responsible for identifying two courses that emphasize ECR taken by each of their majors," Kurata said. "It was up to the departments and programs to identify where their majors would take these courses." Kurata and members of the ECR committee were determined to meet with each chair individually to talk practically about how ECR outcomes could be included in courses. "We found many times that departments were already teaching ECR, but [these goals] hadn't been identified or articulated as objectives before," Kurata said.

To assist departments with this work, the ECR committee developed a matrix with criteria for achieving an ECR designation in a course (see Appendix 5.4). "We had four ECR outcomes altogether, and a course had to address at least two of these four outcomes in a substantial way or begin to address seriously three of the four outcomes in order to be recognized as an ECR course," Kurata said. At a minimum a designated ECR course must be rated as "strong" on at least two learning outcomes or "strong or emerging" on at least three learning outcomes.

Using the matrix, programs and departments submitted applications for ECR designated courses and received feedback on them. In the end, some departments and programs took existing courses and infused ECR components into them, Kurata said, whereas others created new courses.

"For example, we now have a course on chemistry and ethics," Kurata said. "This aligned well with an increasing acknowledgement within the discipline about the ethical and social consequences to chemical research. The faculty who developed this course have published an article on assessment data that demonstrate the significant ECR impact of the course on chemistry majors."

In a similar fashion, the ECR committee engaged departments and programs in the development of capstone courses. From 2008 through 2011, as capstones were developed, faculty members were provided opportunities to present on these courses and build a dialogue across campus. Altogether, more than 25 faculty members presented on their courses and shared materials. As part of the capstone development process, the Core Curriculum Steering Committee, which included the chairs of the ECR committee and two other parallel committees, similarly developed guidelines and a rubric to assist departments and programs (see Appendix 5.5).

Today UAB offers more than 75 ECR-designated courses, and every program has a designated capstone that incorporates and assesses discipline-specific ECR. These programs span arts and sciences, engineering, education, business, health professions, and nursing (see http://www.uab.edu/faculty/resources/item/241-approved-ecr-courses). Overall, Kurata emphasized three main factors that led to the growth of these curricular elements: a shared vision for student learning developed through dialogue; cross-campus engagement and responsibility; and respect for faculty governance and program identity. "We may have encountered some people who thought it wasn't their job [to teach ECR], but we didn't find anyone who said this is not important for students to know," Kurata said. "If you keep the goals central, then you can bring people together to talk about how to achieve the goals. You may not get 100% enthusiasm, but that doesn't mean you won't be successful."

The University of the Pacific: Ethical Autobiography Assignment in General Education

Similar to UAB, the University of the Pacific (Pacific) entered the Core Commitments project at an opportune moment in terms of its educational vision for its 3,900 undergraduates. Just prior to the start of Core Commitments, Pacific had engaged in 3 years of planning that resulted in a new guiding document, *Pacific Rising 2008–2015* (University of the Pacific, 2007b). The document highlighted both enduring core values and aspirational values and reflected "a fundamental and broad institutional commitment to promoting the goals of personal and social responsibility and to funding initiatives that advance these goals" (University of the Pacific, 2007a).

Among six university-wide initiatives laid out in Pacific's Core Commitments proposal, one involved a retooling of the three required academic seminars that form the spine of Pacific's general education program.

Students take the first two of these "Pacific Seminars" (PACS) in the first year and then take the third PACS during their senior year. In this new vision of the PACS, all three would have students grapple with a particular aspect of a new theme for the series, "What Is a Good Society?," with PACS3 serving as an ethical capstone experience appropriate for students in the senior year.

All three of the PACS seminars were designed to focus on ethical issues in relation to the conceptual and practical struggles inherent in defining and building a "good society." The senior-level PACS, in particular, has focused on philosophical, psychological, and religions dimensions of ethics and their application to issues of family, work, and citizenship, pertinent topics for students who were about to face life after college. According to Lou Matz, Pacific's Core Commitments team leader and then director of general education, from the inception of the original course in the mid-1990s, there was a significant reflective component to the course for students to integrate their Pacific experiences and connect them to their future plans.

The PACS seminars are taught by faculty across different departments, but each had common or shared outcomes that transcend individual sections of the course. For PACS3, these outcomes include "articulating one's own moral values and framework," and "applying the course material to an analysis of one's own moral development, moral values, and behavior." For the past 10 years, there has been a common course reader, which is revised every 2 years. During the Core Commitments project, Pacific significantly improved the course reader, especially strengthening the chapters on moral development theories and psychology and ethics. Ethical and moral development theories had been part of the seminar since its inception when planners sought to introduce ethical theories in a way that would have a personal impact on students—through narrative. The narrative focus of the course is reflected in three required assignments: a biography project, reviews of films with ethical themes, and a student ethical autobiography. For the biography project, students choose a biography and analyze the ethical aspects of the person's life. For the film reviews, faculty members assign at least two films, and students analyze the films' ethical dimensions. Finally, students write their ethical autobiographies as the centerpiece assignment of the course. The autobiography assignment is split into two parts: students write the first version of their autobiography at the beginning of the semester and then rework it in light of course materials and discussion. Students are given the detailed assignment and a grading rubric for the first version of the autobiography almost immediately and this version is due to the teacher by the end of the second week of class. They are also given a revised grading rubric—which adds an extra objective to the assignment, "Use of Course Material"—as part of the assignment for the second version (see Appendices 5.6 and 5.7). The rubrics for the ethical autobiography were also developed during the Core Commitments project.

Through the course and particularly this assignment, Matz said, "we wanted students to take stock of who they are morally and be aware of that as they left the university and became active in work, started families, and got involved in communities."

The split approach to the assignment and the fact that it is common across course sections lends itself well to multiple kinds of assessment, which in 2007 was a growing topic of concern nationally and at Pacific. "The [nature of the assignment] shows what students have gained in the course," Matz said. "We've been able to look at students 'pre' and 'post.'" As the director of the PACS, Matz also knew he would be responsible for program-level assessment, and the same grading rubrics that are used for course-level assessment of individual students can be used more broadly for program-level assessment. The PACS3 planning committee was able to look at assessment results across sections, and that process led to faculty becoming more vocal with students about the need to draw connections between course material and their experience in the final autobiography and refining the rubric itself to better communicate expectations to students.

Student course evaluations also indicate that this assignment is one of the most effective in terms of contributing to their learning. Students' qualitative comments about the assignment suggest that reflective nature of the assignment allows them to step outside of their own lives and observe and evaluate their decisions and growth as well as engage more deeply in the course material. "Faculty are also changed by the assignment," Matz said. "It gives faculty a deeper appreciation of students as whole people with life histories."

Conclusion

The goal of this chapter was to provide readers with concrete strategies and useful tools for educating students for PSR. The four campus vignettes and the materials included with each vary a great deal, in terms of level, whether it is program level, course level, or assignment level, and in terms of focus. This is understandable given that the approaches of the different institutions reflected the specific missions, student populations, and goals of each. At the same time, the approaches reflect a common goal of wanting to help students develop into more ethically responsible and astute individuals who took themselves and others into account in their decisions and actions.

The approaches also reflect a common aspiration of pervasiveness with respect to educating students for personal responsibility, which was one of the hallmarks of the Core Commitments Initiative. Within this vision of pervasiveness, students would encounter education for PSR at multiple points throughout the curriculum—in general and specialized education—and cocurriculum (breadth). Moreover, students would encounter this education in ways that engaged them in increasingly sophisticated ways over time (depth). Finally, students would come to perceive the value of learning about PSR throughout the larger institutional culture—in the formal messages and symbols and the informal habits and behaviors of members of the campus (coherence).

At the time of the interviews with team leaders, none of these campuses had succeeded in achieving 100% institutional pervasiveness, and, in the end, this is not really the goal. Rather, these campuses had set pervasiveness in their sights as something to be worked toward, because to do less than that would be to risk marginalization and isolation of their programs before they even launched. Campus environments are dynamic, messy, and always-changing places, and educating students to think and act responsibly toward themselves and others is not possible through one-off, isolated activities. What these vignettes suggest is the need to approach the work by forming robust, shared goals for PSR and a sense of strategy about the kinds of activities that would promote breadth, depth, and overall coherence. The vignettes also suggest the value of connecting programmatic efforts with the complexities of students' own lives and of the larger world as one of the best strategies to create lasting educational impact.

References

California State University Northridge. (2007). *Application to participate in the AAC&U Core Commitments Initiative*. Unpublished.

DeAngelo, L., Hurtado, S., Pryor, J., Santos, J., & Korn, W. (2009). *The American college teacher: National norms for the 2007–2008 HERI Faculty Survey*. Los Angeles: University of California, Los Angeles.

Dey, E. L., & Associates. (2010). *Engaging diverse viewpoints: What is the campus climate for perspective-taking?* Washington, DC: Association of American Colleges and Universities.

Peter Hart & Associates. (2009). National survey of AAC&U members. Retrieved from http://www.aacu.org/membership/membersurvey.cfm

University of Alabama at Birmingham. (2007). *Application to participate in the AAC&U Core Commitments Initiative*. Unpublished.

University of Central Florida. (2007). *Application to participate in the AAC&U Core Commitments Initiative*. Unpublished.

University of the Pacific. (2007a). *Application to participate in the AAC&U Core Commitments Initiative*. Unpublished.

University of the Pacific. (2007b). *Pacific Rising 2008–2015*. Retrieved from http://www.pacific.edu/Documents/provost/acrobat/pacific_rising.pdf

NANCY O'NEILL *is director of learning initiatives and codirector of the Center for Excellence in Learning, Teaching, and Technology at the University of Baltimore. Prior to her current position, O'Neill served as an assistant director of the Core Commitments Initiative at AAC&U.*

NEW DIRECTIONS FOR HIGHER EDUCATION • DOI:10.1002/he

Appendix 5.1. Major Topics in the CSUN Core Commitments Resource Guide

Sample Syllabus Language. Includes brief statements on personal and social responsibility, academic integrity, and class conduct as well as sample contract for students to sign.

Personal and Social Responsibility: Cheating and Plagiarism. Includes prompts related to cheating culture, witnessing cheating, sanctions for cheating, advice to a friend, justifications for cheating, lying to instructors, and misreporting community service hours.

Social Responsibility on Campus. Includes prompts related to classroom climate, group work, trends in academic dishonesty, and the impact of academic dishonesty on students' future plans.

Social Responsibility Beyond Campus. Includes prompts on employment scenarios, roommate conflicts, the environment, conflicting obligations, neighborhood violence, and the moral obligations of candidates for office.

Voting and Elections. Includes prompts on political satire, learning about candidate positions, and being a well-informed citizen.

Debt. Includes prompts on fiscal crisis and stress, rising fuel costs, increasing loans to decrease time to degree, credit card debt, and budgeting and money management.

Discussion Questions for Faculty. Includes questions regarding time spent with students' reflective responses, willingness to incorporate topical issues into courses, and creating a classroom climate that respects diverse opinions and self-expression by students.

The full resource guide is available at www.csun.edu/corecommitments

Appendix 5.2. Sample Prompts from the CSUN Core Commitments Resource Guide

"Consider the Consequences"

If students cheat in college, could this behavior have any consequences in the professional world they will enter when they graduate? What kind(s) of job(s) do you want to have when you finish college? What might the consequences of cheating be in these jobs? Be certain to answer each of the items listed below and provide specific details for readers of your essay in explaining your reasoning.

1. Consequences for you?
2. Consequences for your coworkers?
3. Consequences for the company that employs you?
4. Consequences for society as a whole?

"Group Work"

Your instructor has organized the class into groups, given you a group project, and told you that the group may divide up the responsibilities in any way that all the members can agree upon. Your group has divided the work evenly. But as the project goes on, one member—a student who arrived in the United States only 4 years ago—is not producing work that other members of your group think is as good as theirs. You receive an email from the others, asking you whether it is OK to replace the one student's work, put everyone's names on the project, and turn it in without informing the weaker student of the changes. How would you respond? What issues—for example, honesty or fairness—are involved? What consideration does the weaker student deserve in this situation?

"Voting"

This November, U.S. voters will make a historic choice when they vote for the next president: one that will deeply influence our economy, foreign policy, health care, environment, and many other issues for decades to come. Yet many voters approach this decision armed only with what they can learn from advertisements or late-night comedy shows. They may know even less about the many important races and ballot measures that will also be decided in November. Your roommate, an avid news reader who volunteers for his or her political party, explodes in frustration one day, saying that people who don't know or care about the issues shouldn't have an equal vote with people who have taken the time to read the voter information mailings, visit the candidates' websites, and think through the issues.

New Directions for Higher Education • DOI:10.1002/he

Does your roommate have a point? Write an essay in which you describe what would be the ideal for participation in a democracy—including but not limited to responsible voting. Then identify the things that keep you or people you know from taking on these responsibilities consistently. Finally, explain how society can encourage active and well-informed citizenship, especially among college students.

"Budget"

You are an acknowledged notetaker and generally do well in large GE lecture classes. A friend jokingly suggests that you should sell your notes to people who don't come to class. You can certainly use the extra money because you cannot work any additional hours (although taking notes to sell is, after all, work; think about what it would entail), and you are even beginning to worry about the cost of your commute. What would you do? What ethical problems, if any, do you see in engaging in this enterprise?

Appendix 5.3. Sample Module Titles from UCF's "What Every Faculty Member and Every Student Should Know about Academic Ethics"

Detecting and Preventing Academic Dishonesty (Dr. Nancy Stanlick). This module includes common cheating methods, causes of academic dishonesty, and approaches to preventing academic dishonesty.
Civic and Ethics Education (Dr. Peter Jacques). This module includes a set of propositions to consider ethics education as a part of civics education and includes an extensive case study.
Towards an Ethics for Faculty (Dr. Michael Strawser). This module lays out a framework for faculty ethics in the areas of research, teaching, and service.
Helping Students Learn How to Cite Sources and Avoid Unintentional Plagiarism (Ann Maukonen). This module includes tips for faculty teaching general education courses that do not have writing prerequisites as well as tools to help students understand the ethical use of sources.

For more information, see http://integrity.sdes.ucf.edu/cc/faculty/

Appendix 5.4. UAB Learning Outcomes Matrix for Designated Ethics and Civic Responsibility (ECR) Courses

	Focus on Learning Outcome in Course	
Learning Outcomes	Strong Component is…	Emerging Component is…
4.1. Students understand and practice ethical reasoning and decision making	Discussed and demonstrated in class and is a substantial focus in course materials, assignments, and assessments	Regularly discussed in class but is a minor focus in assignments and assessments OR is intentionally taught by other means and is a significant focus in assignments and assessments
4.2. Students are knowledgeable about contemporary events and/or issues	Discussed and demonstrated in class and is a substantial focus in course materials, assignments, and assessments	Regularly discussed in class but is a minor focus in assignments and assessments OR is intentionally taught by other means and is a significant focus in assignments and assessments
4.3. Students understand civic responsibility	A major focus in course materials, activities, assignments, and assessments	Regularly discussed in class but is a minor focus in assignments and assessments OR is intentionally taught by other means and is a significant focus in assignments and assessments
4.4. Students understand the role and value of diversity	Discussed and demonstrated in class and is a substantial focus in course materials, assignments, and assessments	Regularly discussed in class but is a minor focus in assignments and assessments OR is intentionally taught by other means and is a significant focus in assignments and assessments

Source: http://www.uab.edu/images/degexc/QEP/pdf/2ECR_matrix_template.pdf

Appendix 5.5. UAB Capstone Designation Guidelines (Excerpt) and Rubric

The attached capstone rubric has been developed to help ensure a level of consistency in courses designated as a capstone and specific coverage of targeted QEP competencies. The Core Curriculum Steering Committee will review applications for capstone designation.

For existing courses, submit:

1. Completed capstone rubric as cover sheet with justifications for any exceptions
2. A proposed revised catalog description that indicates the QEP-goal-related content
3. Course syllabus that identifies specific QEP goals among its learning outcomes
4. Copies of any exams and assignments that aren't described in the syllabus

For new courses, submit:

1. Completed capstone rubric as cover sheet with justifications for any exceptions
2. A proposed catalog description that indicates the QEP-goal-related content
3. A proposed course syllabus that identifies specific QEP goals among its learning outcomes
4. A one- to two-page memorandum that describes the plan for assessing the relevant QEP competencies if this is not evident in the syllabus.

Proposed or Existing Course Title:			
Proposed or Existing Course Number: _____ Number of Credit Hours: _____			
If less than 3 credit hours, provide justification:			
The capstone course/experience should	Yes	No	Justification (required for "No" answers) or Comments
Be or be connected to an academic course.			
Be a culminating learning experience that reinforces, integrates, and applies previous knowledge.			
Be based on and reflect the specific approaches, methods, and practices of the discipline.			
Include a set of well-defined learning outcomes and corresponding assessments.			
Reinforce and assess student competencies in discipline-specific writing.			
Reinforce and assess student competencies in discipline-specific quantitative literacy.			
Reinforce and assess one or more ethical issues related to the discipline.			
Facilitate the successful transition from college to a postgraduation life of responsible civic engagement.			
Be completed during the last 30 hours of coursework.			
Be required for graduation in the degree program or degree track.			
Be facilitated and evaluated by full-time experienced faculty.			
Have section sizes no larger than 30 students or have a faculty-student ratio of no more than 1/30.			

Source: http://www.uab.edu/faculty/images/Faculty_Development/QEP/Capstone_rubric_Oct_2008.pdf

Appendix 5.6. University of the Pacific PACS3 Ethical Autobiography Assignment and Grading Criteria, First Version (Abridged)

Describe your ethical identity. In answering this question, address at least the following questions. What are your foundational ethical values? Are there particular ethical issues that are especially important to you? If so, why are they important, and are you able to characterize the underlying principle(s) for your views on them? Which people and experiences or events (direct or indirect) have been the most important influences on your ethics? Consider the influence of your family, friends, teachers, religious leaders, coaches, and others. Consider any social or political events that have been ethically significant for you. Describe any significant ethical situations in which you have been involved and how you responded, or should have responded. As much as possible, give a vivid and detailed description and analysis. Make sure to address the four categories in the grading criteria below.

You can approach your autobiography in any way that makes sense to you, but I encourage you to be creative with the format, not the facts of your life. In the past, students have written about their lives in the form of a letter to a loved one, as a dialogue with a friend or family member, or around an important personal or family theme or event. It's perfectly acceptable, though, to give a straightforward chronological account of your life, too. There is no minimum page length, but it is important to address the categories below in enough detail since my comments on this version will help guide your final version.

Finally, no one will read your autobiography but me. It will be kept confidential. And you will NOT be graded on your life but on how well you address the categories below. While this assignment is required, I hope you frame it as a provocative opportunity to write about your life for your own well-being, and perhaps the well-being of others.

CATEGORY	Excellent = A	Good = B	Fair = C	Inadequate = D
Self-Description	Vivid and thorough description of your ethical self-identity, including your most important ethical values and approaches to ethical decisions	Good, but less vivid and thorough, description of your ethical self-identity, including your most important ethical values and approaches to ethical decisions	Satisfactory but undeveloped description of your ethical self-identity, including your most important ethical values and approaches to ethical decisions	Undeveloped description of your ethical self-identity, including your most important ethical values and approaches to ethical decisions
Environmental Impact	Thorough and thoughtful explanation of the impact of family, friends, role models, important life events, school, activities, religion, culture, etc., on your ethical self-identity	Good, but less thorough and thoughtful, explanation of the impact of family, friends, role models, important life events, school, activities, religion, culture, etc., on your ethical self-identity	Some explanation of the impact of family, friends, role models, important life events, school, activities, religion, culture, etc., on your ethical self-identity, but lacking development and/or analysis	Little or no explanation of the impact of family, friends, role models, important life events, school, activities, religion, culture, etc., on your ethical self-identity
Significant Personal Decisions/Reactions	Thorough and thoughtful description and analysis of significant personal decisions as well as reactions to important life events on your ethical self-identity	Good, but less thorough and thoughtful, description and analysis of significant personal decisions as well as reactions to important life events on your ethical self-identity	Some description and analysis of significant personal decisions as well as reactions to important life events on your ethical self-identity, but lacking development and/or analysis	Little or no description and analysis of impact of key personal choices and reactions to important life events on your ethical self-identity
Writing Quality	Writing is clear and well-organized	Writing is generally clear and well-organized	Writing is generally adequate	Writing might be generally difficult to understand

Appendix 5.7. University of the Pacific PACS3 Final Ethical Autobiography: Instructions and Grading Criteria

The assignment for your final autobiography is the same as the first version *except that you are to incorporate all of the relevant ideas from the course readings and discussion into your revised version in order to frame and describe your ethical autobiography with greater understanding and depth. The goal is to apply the course material to make better sense of your life.* This added component is worth 50% of the grade. I expect that you will substantially rewrite your final autobiography and not simply make minor changes to your first version and insert brief references to the course material. I recommend that you put your first version aside and rethink how you want to approach your final version and then incorporate whatever parts of your first version are serviceable.

Topic:

Describe your ethical identity. In answering this question, address at least the following questions. What are your foundational ethical values? Are there particular ethical issues that are especially important to you? If so, why are they important, and are you able to characterize the underlying principle(s) for your views on them? Which people and experiences or events (direct or indirect) have been the most important influences on your ethics? Consider the influence of your family, friends, teachers, religious leaders, coaches, and others. Consider any social or political events that have been ethically significant for you. Describe any significant ethical situations in which you have been involved and how you responded, or should have responded. As much as possible, give a vivid and detailed description and analysis. You must address the categories in the grading criteria on page two below, making sure to incorporate as much of the course material as is relevant to sharpen and deepen your autobiography. There is no minimum page length, but it is important to address the categories below in enough detail.

When you turn in your autobiography in the supplied file folder, please include the first version of your autobiography with my marked up sheet "Ideas from Readings to Incorporate in your Final Autobiography" so that I can see how much you reworked your first version and whether you addressed the themes on the "Ideas from Readings" sheet.

CATEGORY	Excellent = A	Good = B	Satisfactory = C	Inadequate = D
Ethical Values (Weight = 15%)	Vivid and thorough description of your ethical self-identity, including your most important ethical values, approaches to ethical decisions, and worldview or philosophy of life	Good, but less vivid and thorough, description of your ethical self-identity, including your most important ethical values, approaches to ethical decisions, and worldview or philosophy of life	Satisfactory but undeveloped description of your ethical self-identity, including your most important ethical values, approaches to ethical decisions, and worldview or philosophy of life	Undeveloped description of your ethical self-identity, including your most important ethical values, approaches to ethical decisions, and worldview or philosophy of life
Sources of Ethical Values (Weight = 15%)	Thorough and thoughtful explanation of the impact of family, friends, role models, important life events, school, activities, religion, culture, etc., on your ethical self-identity and philosophy of life	Good, but less thorough and thoughtful, explanation of the impact of family, friends, role models, important life events, school, activities, religion, culture, etc., on your ethical self-identity and philosophy of life	Some explanation of the impact of family, friends, role models, important life events, school, activities, religion, culture, etc., on your ethical self-identity and philosophy of life, but lacking development and/or analysis	Little or no explanation of the impact of family, friends, role models, important life events, school, activities, religion, culture, etc., on your ethical self-identity and philosophy of life
Significant Personal Decisions/Reactions (Weight = 15%)	Thorough and thoughtful description and analysis of significant personal decisions as well as reactions to important life events on your ethical self-identity and philosophy of life	Good, but less thorough and thoughtful, description and analysis of significant personal decisions as well as reactions to important life events on your ethical self-identity and philosophy of life	Some description and analysis of significant personal decisions as well as reactions to important life events on your ethical self-identity and philosophy of life, but lacking development and/or analysis	Little or no description and analysis of impact of key personal choices and reactions to important life events on your ethical self-identity
Use of Course Material (Weight = 50%) Material includes readings on moral development theory, ethical theory, and readings on the domains of family, friends, work, and citizenship	Use of course concepts and theories is excellent in terms of the accuracy, appropriateness, explicitness, and depth in reflecting on and illuminating your ethical values, their sources, and significant ethical decisions	Use of course concepts is good in terms of the accuracy, appropriateness, explicitness, and depth in reflecting on and illuminating your ethical values, their sources, and significant ethical decisions	Use of course concepts is satisfactory in terms of the accuracy, appropriateness, explicitness, and depth in reflecting on and illuminating your ethical values, their sources, and significant ethical decisions	Use of course concepts is inadequate in terms of the accuracy, appropriateness, explicitness, and depth in reflecting on and illuminating your ethical values, their sources, and significant ethical decisions
Writing Quality (Weight = 5%)	Writing is clear and well-organized	Writing is generally clear and well-organized	Writing is generally adequate	Writing might be generally difficult to understand

6

This chapter highlights good practices and lessons learned for infusing social responsibility—contributing to the larger community and taking seriously the perspectives of others—as outcomes of college.

Infusing Social Responsibility into the Curriculum and Cocurriculum: Campus Examples

Robert D. Reason

Two of the five dimensions identified by the researchers at the Association of American Colleges & Universities (AAC&U) who worked on the Core Commitments Initiative can be intuitively classified as "social responsibility" dimensions. This chapter reviews research and good practice related to these two social responsibility dimensions: contributing to a larger community and taking seriously the perspectives of others.

The Core Commitments Initiative

The Core Commitments Initiative at AAC&U focused national discourse on the development of personal and social responsibility (PSR) among students in American higher education. Proponents called for higher education institutions to refocus on PSR as essential outcomes of higher education. After extensive review of the existing literature, Core Commitments project staff identified five broad dimensions of PSR:

- Striving for excellence;
- Cultivating personal and academic integrity;
- Contributing to a larger community;
- Taking seriously the perspectives of others; and
- Developing competence in ethical and moral reasoning.

These dimensions served as the foundation for discussion and assessment for institutions in the Core Commitments project.

NEW DIRECTIONS FOR HIGHER EDUCATION, no. 164, Winter 2013   © Wiley Periodicals, Inc.
Published online in Wiley Online Library (wileyonlinelibrary.com) • DOI:10.1002/he.20076

This chapter reviews the two dimensions that might best be described as "social responsibility" dimensions: contributing to a larger community and taking seriously the perspectives of others. The Core Commitments Initiative described contributing to a larger community as "recognizing and acting on one's responsibility to the educational community and the wider society, locally, nationally, and globally" (Dey & Associates, 2010, p. 1; O'Neill, 2012, p. 3). O'Neill (2012), in a review of empirical research related to this dimension, suggested that outcomes such as civic engagement and awareness, socially responsible leadership, and active involvement in the political process fall under the umbrella of this dimension. Student behaviors such as service learning, community service, and volunteering are recognizable exemplars of this form of social responsibility.

This chapter also focuses on the perspective-taking dimension, which was defined as "recognizing and acting on the obligation to inform one's own judgment; engage diverse and competing perspectives as a resource for learning, citizenship, and work" (Dey & Associates, 2010, p. 1; O'Neill, 2012, p. 3). Again, O'Neill (2012) operationalized this dimension to include many outcomes related to openness to diversity and pluralistic worldviews. Students' engagement with diverse others, particularly engaging in honest discussions across and about differences in race or ethnicity, political orientation, or other forms of personal diversity, is the type of student behavior that demonstrates this dimension.

With these two definitions in mind, we now turn to the research findings that come from the Core Commitments Initiative, focusing first on quantitative results from the Personal and Social Responsibility Inventory (PSRI), the instrument developed to measure the five dimensions of PSR. Following this brief review of findings, the chapter focuses on good practices, from two Core Commitments institutions, designed to influence the development of social responsibility in students.

Review of Existing Research

Much like the general conclusions related to excellence, integrity and ethical and moral reasoning dimensions offered by O'Neill in Chapter 5 of this volume, the findings related to both the commitment to community and perspective-taking dimensions suggest that students and campus professionals agree that these dimensions should be, but currently are not, core outcomes of a college education. The research from the Core Commitments project, as well as other national studies, provides some direction about how to develop these outcomes. Further, and importantly, the research suggests that these two dimensions are related in meaningful ways; that improving the climate for developing along one dimension likely increases development along the other.

Research Related to Commitment to Community. Dey and his associates (2009) found "near-universal endorsement from students and campus professionals" (p. 3) that contributing to a larger community should be a major focus of higher education. Specifically, 93% of students and 97% of campus professionals responding to the PRSI in 2007 agreed or strongly agreed with this belief. However, less than half of these respondents believed that it was an emphasis at their current institution, indicating a considerable gap between the ideal and the reality of educational emphasis on promoting a commitment to community. Interestingly for students, the gap between perceptions of what should be and what is current practice related to promoting a commitment to community actually widens as they progress through school.

Even with increased attention on civic learning and community engagement (McTighe Musil, 2012; National Task Force on Civic Learning and Democratic Engagement, 2012), students may not be engaging in activities known to improve civic knowledge and skills at acceptable rates. Although half of Dey and Associates' (2009) student sample strongly agreed that institutions provided opportunities to engage in civic activities, less than 20% of respondents indicated they frequently participated in course-based community service and less than 30% reported frequently participating in noncourse-based community service.

The lack of engagement in community-based activities may be one reason for some disturbing findings related to civic knowledge reported by O'Neill (2012) in her summary of research. O'Neill reported that only about one-fifth of first-year students and one-third of senior-year students score "high" on a civic awareness measure. These findings reinforce those of Dey and Associates (2009), who reported that only 33% of their respondents indicated "their experiences in college had helped them to expand their awareness of the importance of being involved in the community…, learn the necessary skills to effectively change society for the better…, or deepen their commitment to change society for the better" (p. 21).

The noticeable disconnection between students' desires to focus on contributing to a larger community as part of higher education, their actual behaviors related to civic engagement, and their knowledge about civic issues belies the sense of urgency that led the National Task Force on Civic Learning and Democratic Engagement (2012) to conclude that the United States was at a "crucible moment" (p. 17) related to civic education. The task force called for innovative and comprehensive changes to higher education that would support a civic ethos on campus, ensure that civic literacy is a core outcome for students, infuse and reward the study of civic issues across all disciplines, and advance civic action through community-based partnership. That these recommendations, and the document within which they are discussed, were released in a White House ceremony in January 2012 only reinforces the national importance many attach to civic engagement and learning in American higher education.

Research Related to Perspective Taking. Even as civic engagement and commitment to a larger community have begun to receive greater attention among higher education professionals and federal policy makers, issues of diversity, perspective taking, and the ability to engage across human differences remain important topics. Issues of diversity and representation, especially related to affirmative action in admissions decisions, take up much of the attention of researchers as well as the public.

The United States Supreme Court's decision to hear *Fisher v. Texas* in 2012 placed race-based admissions policies and the representation of racially diverse students on college campuses back in the public spotlight. The research that came about as a result of the previous affirmative action cases involving the University of Michigan, however, demonstrated that it was engagement with diverse others, not simply the presence of diverse others on campus, that mattered to student learning (Gurin, Dey, Hurtado, & Gurin, 2002; Milem, Chang, & Antonio, 2005). The outcomes that emerge from engagement with diverse others, such as pluralistic orientation or openness to diversity and challenge, fall under the dimension labeled "taking seriously the perspective of others" by Core Commitment researchers (Dey & Associates, 2010).

As with the other dimensions of PSR they studied, Dey and his colleagues (2010) found that students and professionals believed strongly that taking seriously the perspectives of others should be a major focus of higher education. Unfortunately, as with the other dimension, the actual institutional focus on perspective taking does not reach the level these respondents believe it should. About 77% of all professionals in the survey and 58% of students believed that institutions should focus on perspective taking, but only 33% of both groups believed that their current institutions did make it a major outcome.

Research suggests that certain activities are related to the development of diversity-related learning outcomes like the ability to seriously consider the perspective of others (Dey & Associates, 2010; Pascarella & Terenzini, 2005). Generally, activities that intentionally and purposefully expose students to diverse ideas or diverse others encourage the development of perspective taking. Dey and his colleagues (2010) found that students who reported more engagement in community service reported greater growth in the ability to analyze and make connections between diverse perspectives. Similarly, students who reported more interaction with faculty members reported that they were more likely to explore controversial ideas or diverse perspectives in their academic work.

The quantitative findings from Dey and Associates (2010) were reinforced by themes that emerged from students' responses to open-ended questions on the PSRI. Students reported that classroom discussions about controversial or provocative topics, especially when faculty members emphasized respecting differing viewpoints, were educationally powerful in the development of students' perspective-taking abilities. Students also reported that interactions with peers within campus climates that support open discussion about differences resulted in greater growth on this dimension.

Relationships Between Commitment to Community and Perspective Taking. The two social responsibility dimensions from the Core Commitments Initiative are certainly not distinct from each other. Hurtado (2007), Hamrick (1998), and Reason (2011) argued convincingly for theoretical and empirical connections among the civic mission of higher education, civic engagement of students, and diversity-related outcomes. Dey and colleagues' (2010) finding that students who reported more engagement in community service reported greater growth in the ability to analyze and make connections between diverse perspectives underscores the relationship between these two dimensions.

Although the connection between engaging with one's community and the development of perspective-taking abilities appears to be well established, we cannot argue that community engagement causes the development of perspective-taking abilities; nor can we argue that perspective taking causes students to engage more with their communities (Dey & Associates, 2010; O'Neill, 2012). The direction of the relationship, although intellectually interesting, matters less for our practical purposes. If institutions of higher education want to encourage students to develop along the two social responsibility dimensions discussed in this chapter, students should be encouraged to participate in community-based service opportunities and provided ample opportunities to engage with diverse others. Both practices are beneficial in their own right, but engagement with one seems to encourage development of the other.

Case Studies from Core Commitments Institutions

Each of the 23 institutions that made up the Leadership Consortium of the Core Commitments Initiative agreed not only to participate in data collection through the PSRI but also to continue and expand institutional efforts to address at least one of the PSR dimensions. Although any number of institutional efforts could be highlighted here, this section provides discussions of two cases meant to serve as exemplars of institutional efforts to further the development of social responsibility among college students: Wagner College's Civic Innovations Program and Sacred Heart University: The Human Journey curriculum.

Although it would be easy, perhaps, to understand the Civic Innovations Program as very good example of an initiative to develop commitment to a larger community and The Human Journey curriculum as an initiative to further perspective taking among college students, these impressions are too simplistic. Although each example illustrates good practice related to its respective dimension, it is more complete to understand each as touching both dimensions. Each campus-based initiative demonstrates the interrelatedness of these two social responsibility dimensions.

Wagner College: Civic Innovations Program. Wagner College is a small, private, 4-year liberal arts college located in Staten Island, New York, with approximately 1,800 undergraduate and 400 graduate students (Wagner

College, n.d.). Wagner also boasts strong connections to its surrounding communities and a long history of positive interactions between faculty and the community. According to Cass Freedland, director of the Center for Leadership and Service at Wagner College at the time of the college's involvement with the Core Commitments Initiative, Wagner also has a long history of course-based community service upon which the Civic Innovations project was built.

The Civic Innovations initiative was developed through a grant from Learn and Serve America and furthered by the work of campus professionals as part of Core Commitments. The Civic Innovations initiative was designed to encourage academic departments to commit to long-term relationships with community partners in the neighborhoods surrounding the campus. Each participating academic department would partner with a single community agency to identify and address the needs of disadvantaged or underprivileged youth. These partnerships allowed for the academic disciplinary expertise of faculty members and students to inform the solutions to community-identified problems.

Each department participating in the Civic Innovations initiative was required to develop new or revise four existing credit-bearing courses within the academic discipline. The content and pedagogical approaches of these courses were codeveloped by faculty members and community partners. According to Freedland, an important outcome of the Civic Innovations initiative was a deeper understanding by faculty members of community-based issues that came about because of the collaborative course development process.

The four courses developed as part of the Civic Innovations initiative were purposefully developmental and intentionally infused with community-based experiential projects. Designers were encouraged to concomitantly increase academic difficulty and practical difficulty as students progressed from course to course throughout their major.

The intentional, developmental combination of curricular and co-curricular experiences for Wagner College students appears to be paying off in engagement with community service. Their own institutional data suggest that the percentage of Wagner students engaged in these activities well outpaces the national average. Wagner reports that 85% of first-year students and 79% of senior-year students have participated in community-based projects as part of an academic course, compared to about 37% of first-year students and 50% of senior-year students nationally (Wagner College, n.d.).

Sacred Heart University: The Human Journey. Sacred Heart University (SHU), located in Fairfield, Connecticut, is a private, Catholic institution that enrolls approximately 3,500 full-time and 700 part-time undergraduate students and 2,200 graduate students. As with many religiously based higher education institutions, the values of the church upon which it was founded influence SHU in meaningful ways. As Michelle Loris, associate dean of the College of Arts and Sciences at SHU explained, the Catholic intellectual tradition permeates all educational efforts at the institution, including the work around the outcome identified by the Core Commitments Initiative.

According to Loris, the Catholic intellectual tradition can be understood as a long-running "conversation" between the church thinkers and the larger culture of contemporary society. The tradition honors intellectual inquiry; combines faith, reason, and Catholic values; and focuses on issues of love, dignity, diversity, the common good, and human rights. This intellectual tradition manifests in SHU's exploration of "The Human Journey."

The Human Journey is a four-course common core curriculum that focuses on four fundamental questions of human existence:

1. What does it mean to be human?
2. What does it mean to live a life of meaning and purpose?
3. What does it mean to understand and appreciate the natural world?
4. What does it mean to forge a more just society for the common good?

These questions are addressed in each of the identified common core courses, a required capstone course that includes a community service component, and a series of lectures throughout the academic year. Students (and in many cases faculty and staff) are encouraged to maintain reflective journals about each of these experiences. During the Core Commitments Initiative, SHU participants were encouraged to connect learning experiences within The Human Journey curriculum to each of the five dimensions of PSR.

According to Loris, the work with AAC&U's Core Commitments and SHU's The Human Journey allowed for integration of curricular and cocurricular experiences for students, which improved student learning in meaningful ways. She gave as an example a one-credit project that arose from the nursing and psychology departments. Interested students in these academic areas attended a retreat that focused on learning along the five dimensions of PSR, and resulted in a project working at a free or reduced-cost health center. Students, throughout their service, reflected in writing on the four fundamental questions, with special focus given to issues of human connection and empathy.

Issues of human connection, empathy, and diversity are also the focus of many of the regularly scheduled lectures that are part of The Human Journey curriculum. These lectures, which include presenters both from within and outside of the SHU faculty, have included topics such as genocide and the bystander effect, hate crimes, the ethics and implications of the dwindling water supply, and masculinity. Students are expected to attend multiple lectures each semester and make connections between the content of the lecture and the four foundational questions.

SHU's The Human Journey, with its multiple components, provides students with shared curricular and cocurricular experiences that require them to grapple with the four fundamental questions, focus on connections and empathy, and articulate perspectives of the human experiences that draw upon multiple academic disciplines and the Catholic intellectual tradition. The faculty and staff at SHU have intentionally created an environment that requires students to engage with diverse others and diverse ideas and, through the active use of reflective writing, come to some integrated understanding of what they have learned.

Lessons Learned

The exemplar cases provide multiple lessons for other higher education professionals who wish to implement programs designed to improve student development of social responsibility. Some lessons come directly from the individuals at the campuses, whereas others arise from the cross-case comparison of the strategies employed and successes reached by each institution. This section touches briefly on some of these lessons.

Support of New Initiatives Is Essential. Involvement with the Core Commitments Initiative came with financial support to implement campus-based projects. Wagner's Civic Innovations initiative started out as a project funded by Learn and Serve America, and campus professionals were able to use Core Commitment resources to augment other financial and human resources to expand existing projects. SHU's The Human Journey curriculum was under way when the call for Core Commitments participants was opened. According to Loris, Core Commitment resources allowed SHU faculty and staff to focus on integrating curricular and cocurricular components like a living-learning community, service learning opportunities, and reflective journaling.

Alignment with Mission Is Fundamental. Connecting The Human Journey curriculum to the Catholic intellectual tradition that informs the mission of SHU allowed for keener focus of activities and greater institutional buy-in among faculty and staff. Similarly, the Civic Innovations initiative was built upon a vision set by the Wagner's president and provost who challenged faculty, staff, and students to become more engaged with the local community. In both cases, the connection between institutional mission and Core Commitment activities sent a message about the importance of and generated enthusiasm for the activities.

Institutionalizing Activities Reinforces Their Importance. The Core Commitment activities at both Wagner and SHU were institutionalized and rewarded at many levels, beyond the explicitly articulated connection to mission at both institutions. Wagner rewarded faculty members' participation in the Civic Innovations activities through stipends and recognition. Significantly, these activities were acknowledged and honored through faculty promotion and tenure processes. The Human Journey was institutionalized for students at SHU because it was part of the core curriculum, sending the message that these activities were important enough to earn academic credit.

New Directions for Higher Education • DOI:10.1002/he

Student Learning Arises from Integrated Activities. Both the Civic Innovations initiative and The Human Journey curriculum integrated curricular and cocurricular activities focused on common goals. The broader issues of PSR, identified as five dimensions by the Core Commitments Initiative, served as a framework to focus the work of these two projects. Focused discussions occurred between faculty, administrators (including student affairs administrators), and community partners to identify educationally meaningful activities. Although these activities may not have necessarily occurred in the classroom, each was intentionally connected to academic learning.

References

Dey, E. L., & Associates. (2009). *Civic responsibility: What is the campus climate for learning?* Washington, DC: Association of American Colleges and Universities.

Dey, E. L., & Associates. (2010). *Engaging diverse viewpoints: What is the campus climate for perspective-taking?* Washington, DC: Association of American Colleges and Universities.

Gurin, P. E., Dey, E. L., Hurtado, S., & Gurin, G. (2002). Diversity and higher education: Theory and impact on educational outcomes. *Harvard Educational Review, 72,* 330–366.

Hamrick, F. A. (1998). Democratic citizenship and student activism. *Journal of College Student Development, 39,* 449–460.

Hurtado, S. (2007). Linking diversity with educational and civic missions of higher education. *The Review of Higher Education, 30,* 185–196.

McTighe Musil, C. (2012). A "national call to action" from the National Task Force on Civic Learning and Democratic Engagement. In D. W. Harward (Ed.), *Civic provocations. Bringing Theory to Practice Monograph Series* (pp. 69–74). Washington, DC: Association of American Colleges and Universities.

Milem, J. F., Chang, M. J., & Antonio, A. L. (2005). *Making diversity work on campus: A research-based perspective.* Washington, DC: Association of American Colleges and Universities.

National Task Force on Civic Learning and Democratic Engagement. (2012). *A crucible moment: College learning and democracy's future.* Washington, DC: Association of American Colleges and Universities.

O'Neill, N. (2012). *Promising practices for personal and social responsibility: Findings from a national research collaborative.* Washington, DC: Association of American Colleges and Universities.

Pascarella, E. T., & Terenzini, P. T. (2005). *How college affects students (Vol. 2): A third decade of research.* San Francisco, CA: Jossey-Bass.

Reason, R. D. (2011). Expanding the conversation: Perspective-taking as a civic outcome of college. *Journal of College and Character, 12*(2). doi:10.2202/1940-1639.1786

Wagner College. (n.d.). *Wagner at a Glance.* Retrieved from http://wagner.edu/about /facts/

ROBERT D. REASON *is associate professor of higher education at Iowa State University and director of the Personal and Social Responsibility Inventory.*

7

The chapter examines the effectiveness and long-term viability of reform efforts designed to advance education for personal and social responsibility.

Strengthening and Deepening Education for Personal and Social Responsibility

Chris R. Glass

This chapter builds on Chapters 5 and 6 of this volume to expand upon the on-the-ground efforts that campuses have used to make significant progress in establishing personal and social responsibility (PSR) as an essential aim of undergraduate education. It discusses the effectiveness and long-term viability of reform efforts designed to advance education for PSR. The chapter explores the conditions and actions that enabled campuses to make education for PSR more deliberate, connected, and pervasive across the student experience (Glass & O'Neill, 2012). The findings come from a case study of seven institutions that participated in the Core Commitments Leadership Consortium. These institutions worked over a 3-year period to expand, deepen, and assess education for PSR on their respective campuses. Integrating PSR became an opportunity for these campuses to invigorate a culture of shared responsibility for excellence in learning, strengthen institutional identity, and deepen a sense of educational purpose. Each campus wove curricular change into the institution's strategic priorities, clearly linking PSR learning with the intellectual skills and knowledge that contributes to academic excellence. More successful efforts used words such as "deepening" and "strengthening" rather than "change" or "reform" in framing their initiatives to key stakeholders.

There is reason for optimism about the potential to revitalize higher education's role in fostering students' PSR. Successful initiatives, nonetheless, are clear eyed about the social, economic, and political realities shaping higher education's strategic priorities: Higher education institutions serve an ever-more diverse student population, they face pressure from

New Directions for Higher Education, no. 164, Winter 2013 © Wiley Periodicals, Inc.
Published online in Wiley Online Library (wileyonlinelibrary.com) • DOI:10.1002/he.20077

83

legislators and administrators to assess student learning, and they strive for position within the competitive higher education landscape. The institutions profiled in this chapter created ways to harness these dynamics to make PSR more pervasive across the student experience. Each institution used the Core Commitments framework as a means to engage a diverse student population, to develop better data collection on campus learning in various forms, and to deepen a distinct set of academic priorities.

Historically, the curriculum is an evolving representation of what faculty believe is necessary for students to know, how developing knowledge is structured, and the kinds of experiences that promote valuable learning outcomes (Bastedo, 2011). Because any one of these features invite multiple interpretations, curricular change evolves through a social process where participants conceptualize, negotiate, and implement a distinct set of academic priorities. This chapter, therefore, provides case examples of what change looked like in different institutional contexts and the social process required in constructing the meaning of each campus's curricular initiatives. It outlines three phases of this social process: finding an entry point, facilitating campus dialogues, and sustaining the work.

Phase 1: Find an Entry Point

In the first phase, campuses identified an entry point for the Core Commitments Initiative. Campus leaders framed a positive agenda for integrating education for PSR, underscoring its relevance to the core academic mission of the institution (Colby & Sullivan, 2009). Educational reform often reflected years of prior work to create more integrated, connected forms of student learning. Campuses used the Core Commitments framework, then, to enhance ongoing initiatives, such as reaccreditation processes or internationalization initiatives. This section uses key phrases from senior administrators' descriptions of their strategic approaches designed to create learning environments that engage the five dimensions of PSR outlined in this volume. Senior administrators described several strategic approaches, including "building bridges," "emphasizing distinctiveness," "identifying gaps," and "reframing resistance." Table 7.1 lists key questions and subquestions that correspond with these administrators' multifaceted approach.

Build Bridges. The success of any institution-wide initiative is influenced by those most intimately involved in leading the effort. Coalition building across reporting lines was a key factor cited by all institutions that agreed their campus had made significant progress. In other words, it mattered "who is in the room" from the inception of the initiative. In building coalitions, campuses purposefully crossed organizational boundaries between student affairs and academic affairs, and among disciplinary areas. Often campuses used existing tried-and-true formal organization groups to consider how to deepen PSR efforts; other campuses, especially campuses

Table 7.1. Key Questions During the First Phase of the Curricular Initiative

Find an entry point	What curricular initiatives already have momentum on our campus?
Build bridges	What groups or individuals should participate in a cross-organizational conversation about PSR?
Emphasize distinctiveness	What elements of the campus mission, history, or commitments resonate with PSR that could frame a positive agenda for change?
Identify gaps	What data does the institution already collect that illuminates student learning related to the various dimensions of PSR?
Reframe resistance	How can the leadership team constructively engage faculty and staff concerns?

needing to reinvigorate efforts, formed new partnerships among people with influence and in positions of formal authority. These individuals possessed tacit knowledge of past change efforts, were familiar with successful and less successful efforts, and were able to generate approaches that their respective constituencies could support.

The most obvious partners in the change process were respected faculty members and senior academic administrators; however, campus leaders also emphasized that deep change necessitated involving leadership "at all levels," including directors of residence adviser training, service learning coordinators, and student affairs professionals. The diversity of perspectives advanced larger institutional goals, and team members benefited from the expansive intellectual community created from multiple points of view on student learning. Frankly, many faculty expressed surprise in learning about student experiences outside of class from student affairs staff, leading faculty to reassess the impact of classroom experiences on student attitudes and behavior. Equally important, teams made significant progress by spending extended periods of time together, such as a half-day or weekend retreat, as opposed to frequent, shorter meetings.

Emphasize Distinctiveness. Successful transformation flowed from efforts that emphasized the distinctiveness of the undergraduate experience at each institution. Although all campuses used the Core Commitments framework designed by the Association of American Colleges and Universities, the process itself created an opportunity for campuses to differentiate themselves from peer institutions. The five-dimension framework provided a catalyst to deepen the institution's historic commitments to education for PSR. Institutions used language rooted in their core values and mission, whether it focused on "educating the whole person," the "Catholic intellectual tradition," becoming an "engaged university," or the "practical liberal arts." The historic commitments of the institution guided conversations in identifying tried-and-true practices that already reflected the institution's commitment to PSR, practices from the past that could be rejuvenated, and "pockets of innovation" occurring on campus that reflected historic commitments in new and creative ways.

Team members also discussed the crucial symbolic role of the university president in linking PSR to larger change efforts already under way. Presidents signaled support by speaking at launch events or formally expressing appreciation for the team's efforts to deepen the campus' historic commitments. In their communications, presidents connected efforts at PSR curricular reform to enhancing student learning. Using the Core Commitments framework became a way to deepen existing curricular capacities, further strategic priorities, and distinguish the institution's undergraduate experience from peer institutions.

Identify Gaps. One of the challenges of PSR educational reform is simply "wrapping your head around what it is." Campus leaders said the five dimensions of Core Commitments provided "a context, a way to talk about some things that were kind of there, but amorphous perhaps." Using the five dimensions offered a framework to understand and assess the campus conditions for PSR. These dimensions allowed the teams charged with instituting reform to advance a positive agenda for change. Teams were able to emphasize where the institution was working toward these learning goals in a meaningful way, as well as identify where more work was needed.

The Personal and Social Responsibility Inventory (PSRI) provided each institution with context-rich data so that the institution could engage in a dialogue and identify existing resources to draw upon in leveraging change. A seasoned institutional researcher, or faculty members with statistical training, helped the team identify and narrow points of interest from the PSRI data. The institutional researcher identified (a) signature strengths where institutional commitment to PSR was visible and well connected; (b) dimensions where there was significant disagreement among student, faculty, and administrators' perceptions; and (c) dimensions with uneven commitment across markers of campus culture (i.e., mission and educational purpose, campus life, curriculum and pedagogy, community and campus partnerships, and incentives and rewards). Some institutions juxtaposed PSRI data with trends from other assessment instruments, such as the Cooperative Institutional Research Project (CIRP) freshman survey, or the National Survey of Student Engagement (NSSE). Institutional researchers found it more manageable to isolate a handful of items, or identify one or two cross-cutting themes; thus, creating a focus for discussions among the various campus constituencies.

Reframe Resistance. Several leaders emphasized how unrealistic it is to expect 100% support "for" any initiative. Equally important, they emphasized that faculty and staff members who had expressed concerns were not necessarily "against" the initiative. As talk of educational reform may evoke the anxieties of faculty and administrators, successful campuses did not interpret this anxiety as resistance per se: "I think every type of change brings out the free-floating anxieties that exist on any campus, and that anxiety attaches itself to any change process. It is important for leaders not to misunderstand that the nature of that anxiety."

Campus leaders viewed the concerns expressed as a starting place for constructive dialogue that could advance the initiative in productive ways (O'Neill, 2006). Sometimes concerns expressed reflected genuine philosophical differences. More often than not, the concerns reflected a desire to be engaged, the perception that the status quo was already working, questions about how the initiative might affect one's role at the institution, or concerns about adding "more commitments" to burgeoning workloads. Several leaders included those persons who expressed the most concern directly on the committee. This ensured these individuals could be engaged in framing and designing the assessment for any new curricular initiatives.

Phase 2: Facilitating Campus Dialogues

In the second phase, campuses facilitated campus dialogues with key stakeholders. Teams worked to identify faculty, staff, organizations, and initiatives on campus whose work related to, or had synergy with, the reform effort. Campuses sponsored campus-wide dialogue where students, student affairs professionals, and faculty discussed issues identified through the PSRI assessment. Discussions based on institutional data (e.g., PSRI, CIRP, and NSSE) were useful when the discussion focused on a discrepancy between what was actually happening on campus and what key stakeholders thought should be happening.

The direction each campus' planning process diverged, taking on the political and social dynamics of the institutional context. Three different contexts provided both the structure and safety to discuss the discrepancies highlighted by institutional data, and the particular challenges their campus faced in fostering students' development of PSR. The campus dialogues described next not only broadened support for the effort, they also led to new cross-institutional connections that helped to sustain long-term reform.

Connecting Pockets of Innovation. Although much progress has been made in advancing diversity practices, such as service learning, intergroup dialogue, and multicultural coursework, these experiences often exist in enclaves within the university. Many campuses discovered that these courses lacked purposeful sequencing within the curriculum. Fragmentation had resulted in students receiving "mixed messages" about the institution's commitment to PSR. Senior administrators described this condition as "hit and miss," "the blind man and the elephant," or "pockets of excellence." Rather than accepting fragmented efforts as inevitable, campuses organized ways to explore or expand cross-campus connections.

Institutions, like Winthrop University, sponsored a 1-day campus conference to engage faculty and student affairs professionals to raise awareness of efforts focused on academic excellence. The Student Excellence, Engagement, and Development Conference "brought together Academic Affairs and Student Life to sow efforts focused on student excellence, student engagement, and student development in the context of our Core Commitments." More than 100 faculty, staff, and student leaders participated in the conference, designed to foster future collaborations within and across divisions. The workshops were not passive experiences for those who attended. Purposeful, mixed seating arrangements facilitated interactions between faculty and student affairs professionals with shared interests in a particular Core Commitments dimension. Faculty and student affairs professionals worked in between these presentation sessions to create new networks among first-year experience, student orientation, and faculty courses to explore how these programs and initiatives could build on and reinforce one another.

Creating a Second Circle of Active Support. Meetings and open forums were common approaches because they involve the typical practices of higher education administrative communication. This approach was highly dependent on maintaining open, transparent communication throughout the process, a history of trusting relationships, and the capacity to negotiate multiple interpretations of the change. Campus leaders explored how they might integrate the new vision for learning into existing efforts:

> One thing that I have learned is that you cannot ever assume that people know what you are doing. Initially, the first couple of years I had a lot of meetings, we had town halls, articles in the paper, and now—over the spring—I met with every single chair. I think there are 66 chairs that I had individual meetings with.

Campus leaders who successfully integrated a vision for PSR on their campuses developed good working relationships with key stakeholders inside and outside the institution and understood the interest of each stakeholder relevant to the change efforts.

The team facilitated conversations with "a second circle of active support," discussing the findings of the PSRI assessment, focusing on what differentiates the institution's approach to the undergraduate curriculum, and exploring connections between reform efforts and existing initiatives. Institutions that pursued this strategy more often described the difficulty with faculty and staff attendance at open forums focused on the curricular reform efforts. Initially, only a handful of people attended the open forums, so campus leaders integrated discussion of the curricular initiative into already scheduled campus meetings.

Cultivating Trust and Collaboration. If the tension between student affairs and academic affairs involved stereotypes or hostilities, institutions sponsored dialogue where each unit could gain a better understanding of the other's contribution to student learning and development. Meaningful action could not take place without first addressing the underlying distrust among divisions. Divisions between academic and student affairs not only created a disconnection that prevented collaboration, the differentiation between the two created an artificial divide among each unit's contribution to student learning and development. Faculty did not understand or appreciate the role of student affairs nor did student affairs understand or appreciate the role of faculty: "We did not appreciate what the other was doing, essentially thinking what we were doing was important to the liberal arts but not what the other was doing." The facilitators designed dialogues to cultivate intergroup understanding, focusing on how each group understood its contribution to student learning: "Instead of talking about the project it was a breaking down stereotypes and team building workshop."

Key Features of Campus Dialogues. The three types of campus dialogues outlined here share some common features. Each type of campus dialogue focused on student learning; a desire to connect existing efforts more coherently; open discussion to understand the action to take in response to the discrepancies highlighted by institutional data; and generating trust in the change efforts among stakeholders. Most important, all of the campus dialogues focused on connecting existing capacities rather than creating something new altogether.

Timing and pacing were critical in the second phase of the curricular initiative. It is vital to note that several administrators confessed they felt they had made little progress after a year's worth of effort! These leaders emphasized, however, that the slowness of the process did not indicate the lack of progress. Rather, moderating the pace of change allowed them to engage a more diverse array of stakeholders in contributing to the process, and, eventually, made implementing reform efforts more successful. As one provost put it: "It took us a long time, but the outcome was substantive, significant change."

Phase 3: Sustaining the Work

In the third phase, campuses developed strategies to sustain the work. Although each campus conceptualized, developed, and implemented educational reform in a variety of ways, each shared a common aspiration of making PSR an essential outcome of an undergraduate education. They shared a desire for students to encounter PSR at multiple points throughout their college experience (breadth) and encounter it in ways that progressively engaged them over the course of their college experience (depth).

The selection of what to emphasize, however, involved making decisions about what not to focus on. Therefore, sustaining the work demanded a carefully delineated focus on how the university would integrate PSR more purposefully into the student experience. Scaling up practices already on campus known for their rigor and effectiveness and expanding those practices were essential for sustainable change.

Integrating Data from Different Assessment Instruments. Successful efforts outlined the change goals, clarified how progress toward new learning goals would be assessed, and described how the data would provide practical guidance for the ongoing development of the curricular initiative. Several campuses realized they already collected data related to PSR outcomes; however, the institution reported these data separately. Senior leaders identified multiple assessments (e.g., CIRP, the Global Perspective Inventory, and NSSE) as part of a "larger mosaic" of student learning: "Our goal has become to view these [assessment] instruments, not as ends in themselves, but as stones in a larger, more meaningful mosaic." Campus leaders identified multiple measures to assess progress related to a particular dimension, for example, contribution to a larger community. Table 7.2 summarizes examples of potential assessment measures for striving for excellence, contributing to a larger community, and taking seriously the perspectives of others (O'Neill, 2012).

Institutions that identified measures for student learning, with regard to PSR, were able to sustain reform efforts. The integration of data from multiple institutional assessments became integral to efforts to move forward provisionally, carefully monitoring progress, assessing the impact of new initiatives, and promising openness to adapting practices if the data did not support the effectiveness of new efforts. The clear connections to institution-wide assessment instruments provided transparency and accountability to those who remained skeptical of the new efforts. The Air Force Academy and Winthrop University, for example, changed the end-of-the-semester student opinion survey to ask students directly about the newly instituted learning goals. If a course was designed to facilitate perspective taking, students now share feedback on how the course helped them make progress along that dimension. For example, the end-of-course survey, in addition to standard items, now includes items such as, "How well did this course help you develop the ability to engage diverse and competing perspectives?"

Cross-Organizational Leadership Positions. One of the most frequently cited accomplishments of successful reform efforts was the cross-organizational communication between student and academic affairs. Prior to educational reform, many campuses felt "organized in pillars" or like "silos and in different worlds." The people involved in the educational reform often wanted to continue the cross-institutional collaboration encouraged by the reform efforts. Several campuses created new units or positions, formed cross-organizational committees, or created leadership

Table 7.2. Examples of Practices and Assessment Measures for Striving for Excellence, Contributing to a Larger Community, and Taking Seriously the Perspectives of Others

	Higher Education Research Institute (HERI)	Wabash National Study
Striving for Excellence		
Engaged Learning Practices	Discussed course content outside of class Communicated regularly with professors	Active and collaborative learning Academic challenge and high expectations Integrating ideas, information, and experiences
PSR Outcomes	Habits of mind for lifelong learning	Academic motivation Need for cognition
Contributing to a Larger Community		
Engaged Learning Practices	Community service as part of a class Volunteering	Community service as part of a class Volunteering
PSR Outcomes	Social agency Civic awareness	Socially responsible leadership Political and social involvement
Taking Seriously the Perspectives of Others		
Engaged Learning Practices	Meaningful and honest discussions about race or ethnic relations with students of other races or ethnicities outside of class Intellectual discussions with students of other races or ethnicities outside of class	Diversity courses Diversity experiences Reflective learning (perspective taking)
PSR Outcomes	Pluralistic orientation	Universality–diversity Openness to diversity and challenge

Source: Adapted from O'Neill (2012).

positions that spanned student and academic affairs (e.g., vice president of student engagement) to ensure ongoing interaction across units and departments. The new positions reflected the kinds of connections academic leaders hoped students would draw upon across their college experience as a whole.

Institutions created new cross-functional units designed to bridge the gap between student affairs and academic affairs, giving more coherence to the student experience. New cross-organizational positions were effective at coordinating oft-fragmented institutional data-gathering efforts on student learning inside and outside of the classroom. They enhanced communication and coordination across academic and student affairs, coordinating initiatives that span traditional boundaries, including student orientation, first-year seminars, service learning, and living-learning communities. Even campuses that did not create new, formal leadership positions maintained informal, cross-campus networks developed through the initiative.

New Course Designations and Sequencing. Campuses also sustained efforts by updating course content, teaching practices, course requirements, or the sequencing of courses. Faculty leadership was central in all of these efforts. Many reform efforts involved updating the course content in learning communities, first-year seminars, and capstone courses to integrate questions of PSR. Others campuses created course-specific guidelines to designate courses that reflected the campuses commitment to specific learning outcomes. The course designations allowed students to select from a variety of courses while ensuring that PSR became more pervasive across the undergraduate experience. The pilot courses also allowed the institution to build examples of what courses that engaged PSR looked like. Pilot courses generated a wealth of assessment data regarding whether such courses produced desired outcomes. None of the campuses spoke in terms of "transformational" change; instead, they emphasized the importance of deliberate, purposeful change that was "slow and small," a "mini-step" where the institution could use assessment data to adapt if the new practices, pathways, or programs did not create the outcomes that had expected.

St. Mary's described their change efforts as "grassroots organizing" forming a faculty advisory group to develop designations for PSR courses along a continuum: (a) a social justice education course that includes attention to issues of justice and equity; (b) a service learning course; and (c) a community-based research course. The University of Alabama at Birmingham (UAB), likewise, wove PSR throughout the undergraduate curriculum as part of its institutional Quality Enhancement Plan. The plan included a minimum of two courses taken in the major that includes civic responsibility, the role of diversity, or ethical reasoning; in addition to a required capstone course that covers "professional ethics, the impact of the discipline on society, and the value of diversity in the discipline." Across the campuses, the new course designations shared these features in common: (a) they rooted PSR in disciplinary habits of inquiry; (b) they anchored students experience through involvement with diverse communities and real-world challenges; (c) they balanced high expectations and support; and (d) they sequenced experiences to provide students appropriate levels of challenge and support as they progressed through their undergraduate education.

Weaving Core Commitments into Campus Communications. Educational reform also provided a symbolic moment for institutions to reaffirm their deeply rooted academic traditions and historic commitments to PSR. Many campuses updated their public relations materials, faculty orientation programs, training of student affairs professionals, and professional development workshops to reaffirm the core values that distinguished their institution's commitment to PSR. Reform efforts became a way to deepen the campus' commitments, distinguishing its undergraduate experience from myriad other options. The process reaffirmed the institutional identity as it worked to attract more students, provide a more engaged education, and reflect the traditions that drew faculty members to join the institution in the first place.

UAB, for example, updated the materials it sends to prospective students, alumni, and supporters to communicate its commitment to ethics and civic responsibility throughout the undergraduate curriculum. A relatively new institution, UAB has a forward-thinking ethos in actively forming community–campus partnerships with nonprofit, government, and community organizations to address issues relevant to the region and state. During the educational reform efforts, UAB received the Carnegie Foundation's elective Community Engagement Classification, recognizing its efforts to serve its region as a civically engaged institution. The updated promotional materials communicated the institution's commitment to partnering with local communities and the greater region as an engaged university.

Final Thoughts

The key lesson from the seven institutions depicted in this chapter, who successfully navigated the currents of change, is this: "Change occurred not necessarily by creating new initiatives but by strengthening connections among existing initiatives as part of a substantive vision for student learning" (Glass & O'Neill, 2012, p. 426). Purposeful connections to student learning are central to successful reform. Derek Bok (2001) describes the consequences of the episodic availability of educational experiences that emphasize PSR:

> We offer many opportunities to our students to prepare for citizenship, but they are only opportunities. Like so much else on campus, learning and

preparing to be a citizen is only an option like singing in the glee club or joining the gymnastics team. But citizenship, of course, is not an option. (p. 2)

Successful efforts, as demonstrated by the seven institutions, provide opportunities for students to integrate learning for PSR across experiences.

The change process outlined in this chapter could seem painfully slow. Many scholars assert the need for fundamental, transformative change. Transformational change is needed; however, no campuses in the case study framed on-the-ground educational reform efforts using the language of transformation. Campus leaders were, however, optimistic about the potential for higher education institutions to develop successful change efforts. Those most closely involved in the change efforts believed incremental change over time had created significant, lasting impacts.

References

Bastedo, M. N. (2011). Curriculum in higher education: The organizational dynamics of academic reform. In P. G. Altbach, P. J. Gumport, & R. O. Berdahl (Eds.), *American higher education in the twenty-first century: Social, political, and economic challenges* (pp. 409–432). Baltimore, MD: Johns Hopkins University Press.

Bok, D. (2001). *Universities and the decline of civic responsibility*. Tallahassee, FL: Institute on College Student Values.

Colby, A., & Sullivan, W. M. (2009). Strengthening the foundations of students' excellence, integrity, and social contribution. *Liberal Education, 95*(1), 22–29.

Glass, C. R., & Neill, N. O. (2012). Educational reform related to personal and social responsibility: The case of Core Commitments. *Journal of General Education, 61*(4), 406–432.

O'Neill, N. (2006). *Resistance: Not always the enemy*. Retrieved from http://www.aacu.org/core_commitments/documents/Resistance.pdf

O'Neill, N. (2012). *Promising practices for personal and social responsibility: Findings from a national research collaborative*. Washington, DC: Association of American Colleges and Universities.

CHRIS R. GLASS *is assistant professor in the Higher Education Program, Darden College of Education, Old Dominion University.*

INDEX

Reform efforts to advance PSR, effectiveness of, 83–94
Research Institute for Studies in Education (RISE), 7, 44
Responsible person, definition of, 29
Rest, J. R., 20
Roberts, K., 33
Roksa, R., 28, 29
Rudolph, F., 13, 16, 20
Ruff, L., 3, 43
Ryder, A. J., 1, 2, 13, 22, 31, 48

Sacred Heart University, Human Journey curriculum at, 77, 78–80, 81
Sanders, J. R., 37
Santos, J., 10, 50
Saunders, K., 37, 38, 39, 40
Sax, L. J., 34
Schuh, J. H., 37, 42
Seguine, J., 16
Shelley, M. C., 41, 42, 45
Shenkle, C. W., 32
Snyder, R. S., 32
Spencer, M. G., 32, 33, 34, 35
Stanlick, N., 54, 55, 64
Stodden, R. A., 33, 34, 35, 36
Strawser, M., 64
Student values: and behavior, 26–28; exploring, 23–26
Studying, time spent, 28, 29
Sullivan, W. M., 16, 84
Suskie, L., 42
Swenson, A., 52, 53

Terenzini, P. T., 16, 17, 19, 20, 76
Texas, Fisher v., 76

Tierney, W. G., 32, 33
Torres, V., 38
Trosset, C., 2, 15, 23, 29, 30

Umbach, P. D., 38
University of Alabama at Birmingham (UAB), ethics and civic responsibility (ECR) courses at, 55–57, 65–67, 92
University of Central Florida (UCF): academic integrity modules at, 54, 64; faculty development at, 54–55; Z grade designation at, 53–54
University of the Pacific, ethical autobiography assignment at, 57–59, 68–71
Urdan, T. C., 41

Values, student: and behavior, 26–28; exploring, 23–26
Voting, 1, 15, 19, 62–63

Wabash National Study, 18, 23, 25, 27, 29
Wagner College, Civic Innovations Program at, 77–78, 80, 81
Wall Street practices, troubling, 15
Walvoord, B. E., 37
Whitcomb, M. E., 38, 41, 45
Wohlgemuth, D. R., 40
Worthen, B., 37
Writing Reading Across Disciplines (WRAD), 53

Z grade designation, at University of Central Florida, 53–54
Zeller, R. A., 39

NEW DIRECTIONS FOR HIGHER EDUCATION

ORDER FORM SUBSCRIPTION AND SINGLE ISSUES

DISCOUNTED BACK ISSUES:

Use this form to receive 20% off all back issues of *New Directions for Higher Education*.
All single issues priced at **$23.20** (normally $29.00)

TITLE	ISSUE NO.	ISBN
_____	_____	_____
_____	_____	_____
_____	_____	_____

*Call 888-378-2537 or see mailing instructions below. When calling, mention the promotional code JBNND
to receive your discount. For a complete list of issues, please visit www.josseybass.com/go/ndhe*

SUBSCRIPTIONS: (1 YEAR, 4 ISSUES)

☐ New Order   ☐ Renewal

U.S.	☐ Individual: $89	☐ Institutional: $311
CANADA/MEXICO	☐ Individual: $89	☐ Institutional: $351
ALL OTHERS	☐ Individual: $113	☐ Institutional: $385

*Call 888-378-2537 or see mailing and pricing instructions below.
Online subscriptions are available at www.onlinelibrary.wiley.com*

ORDER TOTALS:

Issue / Subscription Amount: $ _____

Shipping Amount: $ _____
(for single issues only – subscription prices include shipping)

Total Amount: $ _____

SHIPPING CHARGES:

First Item	$6.00
Each Add'l Item	$2.00

*(No sales tax for U.S. subscriptions. Canadian residents, add GST for subscription orders. Individual rate subscriptions must
be paid by personal check or credit card. Individual rate subscriptions may not be resold as library copies.)*

BILLING & SHIPPING INFORMATION:

☐ **PAYMENT ENCLOSED:** *(U.S. check or money order only. All payments must be in U.S. dollars.)*

☐ **CREDIT CARD:**   ☐ VISA   ☐ MC   ☐ AMEX

Card number _____ Exp. Date _____

Card Holder Name_____ Card Issue # _____

Signature _____ Day Phone _____

☐ **BILL ME:** *(U.S. institutional orders only. Purchase order required.)*

Purchase order # _____
  Federal Tax ID 13559302 • GST 89102-8052

Name_____

Address_____

Phone_____ E-mail_____

Copy or detach page and send to: **John Wiley & Sons, One Montgomery Street, Suite 1200,
San Francisco, CA 94104-4594**

Order Form can also be faxed to: **888-481-2665**

PROMO JBNND

Statement of Ownership

Statement of Ownership, Management, and Circulation (required by 39 U.S.C. 3685), filed on OCTOBER 1, 2013 for NEW DIRECTIONS FOR HIGHER EDUCATION (Publication No. 0271-0560), published Quarterly for an annual subscription price of $89 at Wiley Subscription Services, Inc., at Jossey-Bass, One Montgomery St., Suite 1200, San Francisco, CA 94104-4594.

The names and complete mailing addresses of the Publisher, Editor, and Managing Editor are: Publisher, Wiley Subscription Services, Inc., A Wiley Company at San Francisco, One Montgomery St., Suite 1200, San Francisco, CA 94104-4594; Editor, Co-Editor Betsy Barefoot, EdD, Gardner Inst. for Excellence in Undergrad. Education, Box 72, Brevard, NC 28712; Managing Editor, Co-Editor Jillian Kinzie, 1900 E. Tenth, Suite 419, Indiana Univ. Center for Postsecondary Research, Bloomington, IN 47405, . Contact Person: Joe Schuman; Telephone: 415-782-3232.

NEW DIRECTIONS FOR HIGHER EDUCATION is a publication owned by Wiley Subscription Services, Inc.,111 River St., Hoboken, NJ 07030. The known bondholders, mortgagees, and other security holders owning or holding 1% or more of total amount of bonds, mortgages, or other securities are(see list).

	Average No. Copies Each Issue During Preceding 12 Months	No. Copies Of Single Issue Published Nearest To Filing Date (Summer 2013)
15a. Total number of copies (net press run)	686	598
15b. Legitimate paid and/or requested distribution (by mail and outside mail)		
15b(1). Individual paid/requested mail subscriptions stated on PS form 3541 (include direct written request from recipient, telemarketing, and Internet requests from recipient, paid subscriptions including nominal rate subscriptions, advertiser's proof copies, and exchange copies)	267	254
15b(2). Copies requested by employers for distribution to employees by name or position, stated on PS form 3541	0	0
15b(3). Sales through dealers and carriers, street vendors, counter sales, and other paid or requested distribution outside USPS	0	0
15b(4). Requested copies distributed by other mail classes through USPS	0	0
15c. Total paid and/or requested circulation (sum of 15b(1), (2), (3), and (4))	267	254
15d. Nonrequested distribution (by mail and outside mail)		
15d(1). Outside county nonrequested copies stated on PS form 3541	3	2
15d(2). In-county nonrequested copies stated on PS form 3541	0	0
15d(3). Nonrequested copies distributed through the USPS by other classes of mail	0	0
15d(4). Nonrequested copies distributed outside the mail	0	0
15e. Total nonrequested distribution (sum of 15d(1), (2), (3), and (4))	3	2
15f. Total distribution (sum of 15c and 15e)	270	256
15g. Copies not distributed	416	342
15h. Total (sum of 15f and 15g)	686	598
15i. Percent paid and/or requested circulation (15c divided by 15f times 100)	99%	99.2%

I certify that all information furnished on this form is true and complete. I understand that anyone who furnishes false or misleading information on this form or who omits material or information requested on this form may be subject to criminal sanctions (including fines and imprisonment) and/or civil sanctions (including civil penalties).

Statement of Ownership will be printed in the Winter 2013 issue of this publication.

(signed) Susan E. Lewis, VP & Publisher-Periodicals